MW01223424

EDOH STEPHEN OWOICHO

A new Dawn

Seventh edition

This book was professionally typeset on Reedsy.
Find out more at reedsy.com

Dedicated to all!

Contents

Preface

There is no qualm to the fact that we all desire the good things of life. Life transit in styles. However, just a few persons have maximise their existence, effectively.

Year's back, as a young lad I used to wake up each new day, asking myself questions. And one of the surprising queries that pop up in my head was this, "when is the sun going to stop shining?" Hmm, I guess those thoughts result from ignorance. But do you know till this very day, the answer never came? Yes, because it's a phenomenon on its own.

A new dawn is a fresh onset glowed by joy. Everyone wants to relish the stunning moments of life. Still, some find it inconceivable.

One misstep, most people's senses is this; discerning the negative occurrence prevailing as the will of God for their life, and it not true.

The Divine Father plans greatly for His Sons and Daughters. He loves everyone equally! Without a doubt, God wants us to experience the fullness of joy.

In life, there are three major phases, every individual must journey through, to fulfil a purpose. It doesn't matter if you were born with a silver spoon. Just as the aforesaid recalls, truly, there are three phases! And here, there is: "The phase of struggle, The phase of restructuring and finally, The phase of exploit."

Truly, in this edition, you'll be delving deep into stunning mysteries that will give you a quantum lift. Also, you'll be able to scale through the phases of life. Recall that in life, you must go through various phases just as the aforementioned stated. Though, men fail in the phases of life because they lack knowledge on how to win.

This book has been put in place by God for your promotion. See it as a divine occurrence, accept it as God sent, and read it like the best literature, you dream if always.

Thank you and God bless you, as you embark on your journey to a New Dawn.

Acknowledgement

ACKNOWLEDGEMENT

I am so grateful to the Celestial King for His delightfulness, support, grace, insight, health, divine preservation and vigour to write this book.

I remain humble to my dad, Mr Reuben Edoh, and my mum, Judith Edoh, Mrs. Too, I want to appreciate my Siblings; Collins Edoh, David Edoh, and Divine Edoh for their prayers, support, and wishes in the course of putting together this book.

I must not fail to recognize the body of Christ for their glorious support. Indeed, I wouldn't get closer to achieving my goals without their prayers and support spiritually.

My gratitude also goes to friends I met in the cave of Adullam; a place of intimacy and fraternity with entities in Zion. I'm grateful to my close friend and brother, Pastor Josiah Onuh for his prayers and wishes. He is indeed, a great person.

To my colleagues at the College of Health Science, Benue State University, Makurdi, Nigeria, I remain grateful for your prayers and especially. Not forgotten friends such as Paul Otokpa, Marvellous Iyanya, Wilson Ochugwu, and the hosts of others. I really appreciate your kind gesture.

I remain grateful to Words Citadel Family for the privilege bestowed on me. Indeed, it's a platform that has given hope to the broken-hearted, depressed, and those suffering from low esteem level. May the good God bless, Words Citadel Family.

Let me not leave the team those who are a direct beneficiary of my previous books. For all of you, I lack words to convey my deep sense of gratitude.

May God bless and reward all of you for your prayers. Amen!

Stephen Edoh

Chief Executive Officer, Words Citadel Family.

I

The phase of struggles

One

The Storms of Life

When you saw the title of this chapter," The Storms of life," you probably thought: well, duh everybody has face one!

Most people haven't walked through the storms of life. I have!

The storms of life aren't the normal storm, we experience, while we stay close to the river, but the one that has to do with psychological and spiritual state of a man.

Every path to glory has it's designed to storm. You might once have asked yourself why all this suffering all in the name of success?? Listen, beloved, that's isn't suffering, it is a battle you will have to fight and win.

Looking back to the past, l extol God for the grace to stand still in different storms, I've fought through and triumph.

In life, every storm is a bridge between here and there. You must always have the burning desire to leave where you are, to a place of luxuries. But you must be ready to face and conquer every giant (storm) of here to get there (place of luxuries).

I too walked through deadly storms like loss of memory, tumour, etc. It took the grace of God to prevail. It was unfortunate, some who just met us thought, all things just work together without a story headline.

The Storm is a major key in understanding the mysteries of time and season. The Bible book of Ecclesiastes 3 makes us understand the mysteries of times and season. Every season has its storm, as I earlier said.

Walking through every storm demands a lot of from you being patient, having the capacity to endure and maintaining a high level of the Jesus mind-set to triumph.

Being Patience in the storm.

There's this famous African adage, the patience Dog eats the fattest bone.

Patience is the greatest in the Family of Mr and Mrs Value. It entails a spirit of total calmness, cool tracked with time, excluded Hastiness.

Patience is a Destiny pathway, this pathway opens up to those who respect the word, wait.

I will define the term "wait" as a phenomenon that demands an ugly agreement to a certain decision. Bhat needed quick attention.

Imagine the case of Hannah, who kept going to Shiloh year after the year ended up with her Samuel. Do you see?? Wonder what will have to happen if she has quit the go. Patience pays.

Endurance

The Oxford advanced learner's dictionary defines the term "endurance" as the ability to continue doing something painful without complaining.

In life, endurance must be embraced if one will walk through the storm.

The storm love people who murmur a lot, it cheers when people exclaimed that mind-set. You need to endure through every dark path.

You need to endure, to enjoy.

Endurance is a big step to achieving greater things. Nelson Mandela's long walk to freedom was an obvious result of endurance.

Same goes to John Wycliffe of blessed memory, who translated the bible from Greek to English. Endured the struggle dear, it's only for a while, weeping last only for a night but joy cometh in the morning, Psalm 30:5.

Having the Jesus mind-set. Amazing!

This flashback to biblical times of our Lord Jesus Christ.

The mind-set of Jesus was an amazing one. His level of faith was superb. Earlier in the Bible book of Isaiah, he made it clear to us "I have made you. I will carry you; I will sustain you and I will rescue you." — Isaiah 46:4.

So have it in mind, he is with you in the storm. Look at this. One day, Jesus said to His disciples, "Let's cross over to the other side of the Sea of Galilee." So these experienced fishermen did what they had done hundreds of times.

They boarded their boat and rowed together while Jesus went below deck and took a much-needed nap.

Suddenly, a severe storm came and dumped rain on them and caused the sea to pitch. It was so bad that these seasoned sailors panicked. They awoke Jesus and said accusingly, "Do You not care that we are perishing?" Jesus silent their criticism and then rebuked the storm, and it stopped immediately. He also rebuked them with these words, "Why are you so fearful? How is it you have no faith?" (see Mark 4:35-40). A better translation of those words says, "Why are you such fearful ones?" Jesus was saying, "Boys, have you learned anything here?", what did Jesus say to them? He said, "Let's cross over to the other side!" He did not say, "Let's go to the middle of the Sea of Galilee and drown together!" If He had said that, they might have been justified in their collective panic.

Jesus did not promise smooth sailing, but He promised a safe passage. I would rather be in a storm with Jesus than anywhere else without Him.

So, therefore, if you are in a storm of life, my advice to you is to remember that Jesus will "get you to the other side." Trust Him, he will not abandon or let you down.

Summary

* Life is full of problems, challenges, limitation, and difficulties. But we must face every situation with the Jesus mind-set.

* Endurance is the key. When we endure the storm whirlwind on us after a while comes the breeze and light of a new dawn.

* The ability to keep calm, while the results get better define patients. Life in the Storm demands a lot from an individual capacity to be calm in the darkest of the moment, also to avoid going down in tears.

* The positivism mind-set is what an individual need in the Storm, he or she should always have it in mind, like the psalmist quoted in Psalm 30:5 "Weeping may last only for a night, but joy cometh in the morning."

To support Stephen Edoh's ministries, kindly forward your assistance to the PayPal address below:

PayPal: stephenedoh2000@gmail.com

PayPal.me/Stephenedoh

Two

The beauty phase of life

Daily, we keep hearing the word "life". But has it meaning ever come to our thinking? No, I probably guess. Life entails a period, that distinguishes a vital and functional body from being a dead one.

At first, we were all Foetus in our mother's womb, before driving down to this planet, Earth, where we all tasted our first breath. Metamorphosis came in, noting the transformation that took place in our lives; from being a kid to become a teenager, down to the very moment, we sailed to adulthood.

Life is beautiful, outstanding and amazing. It is full of accolades, treasures, and glamour's. The beauty phase of life describes the gorgeousness, fairness and loveliness life carries.

It's sound disastrous. Whenever the saying, "life is unfair" caught up with my hearing mechanism. Life is not the bed of a rose, but this doesn't define life to be unfair.

The chronicle of success, begin from the thoughts an individual had towards life. That you struggled yesterday, doesn't mean you will, today.

As noted earlier in this book, life is full of storms, but in this same storms, beauty is found. What differentiates the storms of life, from the beauty phase of life, is the struggle, endurance, and patients in that dimension, while prosperity, breakthrough, and success are the factors that differentiate the beauty phase of life from the storms of life.

A woman who laboured in her travail experienced the storm of life, while the woman who just put to birth, experience, taste and enjoy the beauty, life carries. Forget the period where you struggled, It's a new dawn to move forward, a new dawn for exploits, a new dawn to soar!

Ask a successful man in his 70s, concerning the struggle he had faced, the phases he has journeyed through, and the path he took to a new dawn. He could reply this way, "The latter was better than the former". How does he mean? That will be your question. His response implies that the former days were moments of sacrifice, pain, hard work, etc. While the latter-day here entails the season of harvest, the period of joy, etc.

In life, there are three basic and fundamental phases; The phase of the struggle, the phase of restructuring, and finally the phase of exploit.

THE PHASE OF STRUGGLE

You will surely face difficulties in every dimension of Life. For you to triumph, struggle — Stephen Edoh

The phase of struggle is the dimension, where individuals learn to face the afflictions, adversaries, anguish, and excruciation that are witnessed in life.

The struggles are there to strengthen you. Unfortunately, most of those, in this very phrase, think of it as an apocalypse.

Have you been to a gold mine before? If probably, No is going to be your answer, I'll urge you to go visit one or browse about it. Imagine the labour the miners go through, think of the pain they experience while digging in the quest for gold. Sometimes, luck slips out of their hands. How do I mean? This very statement implies that at most times the miner's search for gold proves abortive.

What will be your advice to the gold-miner, after his labour proved abortive? Maybe giving up the job in search of something productive. But the fact is this, the gold-miner understood the mystery of struggle, he realises at most times; the star doesn't shine, what star? His luck.

Remember, you're on earth for an assigned purpose. Do not let the struggle to bring you down, rather, let it motivate you to move forward. The struggle you faced daily is a setup made to stop you from stepping on the bridge that leads to a new dawn.

The path that leads to the beauty phase of life is overshadowed by a tsunami, a path full of thorns and beasts of no nations.

I firmly believe and affirms to the fact that, if everyone looks at the phase of the struggle, as a phase of preparation, then the proposed journey to a new dawn, get a backing.

I marvelled, each time I see people moving back and forth, after which they end up failing to understand the phase of struggle. The fact is crystal clear: when you cannot sit and analyse the reason, while you're still in bondage, you then create a room for pain. It's time you remove every vestige of trepidation.

"Know this, your struggles are the launching pads to your greatest ever promotion," — Joseph Prince.

Now, walk with me, as I show you the way to go through in the phase of struggle. The first nugget I will emphasise on is;

1. THE SPIRIT OF UNDERSTANDING

"One of the greatest miracles that could take place in the life of an individual is the miracle of understanding" — Joshua Selman.

Prob 3:13 RSV Happy is the man who finds wisdom and the man who gets understanding.

Understanding is the ability to comprehend, also the power to make experience intelligible by applying concepts.

Most times people failed to advance forward, for lack of understanding. Understanding is a basic and fundamental key in pushing through.

To every situation, there is a solution, and also to every equation, there is a formula. Perhaps this is the opposite with others. You could find individuals who have invested their total time in reading, but still not understood all they've read, even when they know the formulas. Same too applies to those struggling in this very phase.

Frankly, the only way to escape incomprehension is by praying. Praying for what? The spirit of understanding.

When an individual goes before the father, and asks for the spirit of understanding, I grant it unto him or her. It's the spirit of understanding that enables an individual to comprehend, make experience intelligible, etc.

Therefore, an individual must fully understand the fact that struggles in this phase are steps on the staircase to a new dawn.

I'm so happy that you're reading this book today. Don't see it as a coincident but a divine appointment set up by God for you.

2. UNDERSTANDING GOD'S PLAN FOR YOU

Jeremiah 29 vs 11 RSV.

For I know the plans I have for you, says the LORD, plans for welfare and not for evil, to give you a future and a hope.

We were all made to understand that God created us in His own image and likeness. Also, the scripture in the previous paragraph made it crystal clear of the plans God has for us. As far, you're a living soul, God has a plan for you. He didn't send you on earth purposeless, but to fulfil a mandate.

It's unfortunate that many forget the fact of

God's plan for them. Some even suggest that God has forgotten them in their struggle, but this isn't true.

Irrespective of the condition you are facing; God's plan for you still stands superior. Men like Joseph, David, and Moses understood God's plan for their life. Think of Joseph, who was sold into slavery for hatred from his brother. But this was a setup. Joseph understood God's plan for him and his family. Even while he was in Egypt, the Bible made it know to us that; he was prosperous in all his ways, up to the very point, His master's wife lust after him, only for her to request of him sex, of which he rejected. It's didn't stop there.

He was thrown into the prison, even when he wasn't guilty of the offense that took him there. We all know this story. To put everything into a summary, the story of Joseph changed. He left the prison to the palace, leaving the dunghill to Capitol Hill, moving to White House from Out House. Oh, my… What an interesting story!

What if Joseph had compromised his faith and submitted to the request of Potiphar's wife? The plans of God wouldn't have fulfilled in His life, and He would have remained a slave until he dies. It is advisable for us to know this, God has a plan for us, and he wants to give us an expected end, i.e. a greater end.

Remember, endurance and patience are the key, as emphasised in the previous chapter. Therefore, Keep calm and endure, because God is working on your blueprint, fixing your future in you for you to have an expected end.

You don't have to compromise, due to the condition you find yourself. Stealing, prostitution, pick-pocketing, gambling won't make a good different, but stopped God's plan for fulfilling in your life.

Just keep working hard, ensure you balance the equation with prayer, and then watch the odds change in your favour.

THE PHASE OF RESTRUCTURING

"God will never take you out of the storm, without making you to understand the mysteries of struggles in the storm," — Stephen Edoh.

The phase of restructuring is a dimension, where an individual come into alignment. It is very significant to note that, at any point in life, eventually, you will undergo a restructuring test.

Unfortunately, most people has failed to accept learning as a pivotal tool, while struggling in life. You must be restructured, before you can advance to the beauty phase of life. How do I mean? You must accept a change in your behaviour, mind-set and ways of life.

Merriam Webster's dictionary, define the term "Restructuring" as a change in the structure of something. It's could be a change in character, a change in the Constitution, perhaps even a change in the way of life, etc.

God wants you to learn something in your struggle, before he takes you out. This is because, at any point, you could come in contact with a storm mightier than the former, you once faced. How do you go about this, when you lack the basic? I guess you give up. But when you stay calm and act with full courage in the storm, your spirit man matures, and your mind-set, as well as enlarged.

Earlier, we could lens through the story of Joseph, and how that God took him from the phase of the struggle to the phase of restructuring, where he became mature. It wasn't a simple thing to reject the request of the wife, to the Chief of Army staffs of a particular Nation. Because, fear alone will overshadow you, not just the fact that she was the wife to the Chief of Army staff, but because of the request she made. What kind? A bad one!

Unfortunately, many will have accepted her request because of fear of losing their life, or perhaps for the sake of favour, etc. But this young man understood the phase God was taking him through. He needed to learn more, get himself positioned and aligned to God's plan, also he needed to get matured, in other to handle future glory.

"Compromise and unnecessary hastiness won't produce a lasting success," — Stephen Edoh.

I go down in tears whenever I see young people, especially youth getting involved in illegal nor ungodly activities, in the name of success. Let me brighten your understanding, "you will never get to the top if you are in haste to succeed."

Success is not an occurrence of hastiness, but a result produced from the mind. Only a restructured mind experience success, produce results, and of all, explodes to the sight of men.

It's time you go get restructured because it pays!!

REASONS AN INDIVIDUAL MUST BE RESTRUCTURED

1. FOR ALIGNMENT

2. FOR MATURITY
3. FOR THE PURPOSE OF UNDERSTANDING VISIONS AND ASPIRATIONS

THE PHASE OF EXPLOIT

1 Sam 18:14 RSV. "And David had success in all his undertakings; for the LORD was with him,"

Exploit is a result produce from two basic factors;

*Understanding and Alignment.

No man successfully triumph over the struggles of life, without understanding and alignment.

The phase of exploit is the phase of reward. You get rewarded after working hard, striving, striking, etc. Everyone wants an accolade in their gallery's, but it results from the understanding of God's plan, and restructuring of the mind, character, etc.

The beauty phase of life is a dimension define by term exploit. In this phase, you are meant to reign, excel and rule. Suffering is a thing of the past, because you've paid the ultimate price.

You can't find compromising people doing exploit, only aligned individuals do exploits. You might ask, but Mr Steve, are there not corrupt people who are rich? Very good, the fact is this: exploit isn't about riches; it entails so many features like, good health, dominion, fame, success, etc. But with those corrupts individuals, it's a different. Some of them are rich in finance, but poor in health. Only those who are clean and uncompromising do exploits.

Poverty, setbacks, limitation in progress, etc are all aliens in this phase. They aren't found in this very dimension of life. When David become king, did he ever went back to the farm? No!! But today you could witnessed prosperity in the life of corrupt individuals, only to discover awhile later, they became poor. Why?

Because success that results from hastiness and compromise, do not last.

Always do the right thing at all times, because it's the key that leads to exploitation. While some are complaining about the fact that life is bitter, some are there busy exclaiming how sweet life is, because of their uncompromising attitude.

I know you've learnt a lot, but more is coming as you keep fighting on your walk to a new dawn.

Be noted, this chapter is just a summary of this book. You will come to understand the phase of struggle, the phase of restructuring and the phase of exploit in the remaining chapters of this book.

You're a generation of exploitation, a royal priesthood and a chosen nation, c'mon It's your time, Shine!!

SUMMARY OF THE BEAUTY PHASE OF LIFE

1. Life entails a period, that distinguishes a vital and functional body from being a dead one.

2. In life, there are three basic and fundamental phases; The phase of the struggle, the phase of restructuring, and finally the phase of exploit.

3. understanding is the ability to comprehend, also the power to make experience intelligible by applying concepts.

4. Compromise and unnecessary hastiness won't produce a lasting success.

5. Success is not an occurrence of hastiness, but a result produced from the mind. Only a restructured mind experience success, produce results, and of all, explodes to the sight of men.

To support Stephen Edoh's ministries, kindly forward your assistance to the PayPal address below:

PayPal: stephenedoh2000@gmail.com

PayPal.me/Stephenedoh

Three

Keep fighting

Every living thing on earth must fight to survive.

Fighting is an advanced process in the metamorphosis of every life carrier organism, including plants. In the life cycle of a housefly, for example, existence begins when a larva hatches from an egg. The larva develops into a pupa and then transitions to the ultimate stage, the adult stage.

This brief metamorphosis is a transparent state of fighting and triumph.

The many stages transcended from birth to death, are beautiful, but demand a high level of continual persistence and perseverance to achieve optimum success.

As noted earlier in the first chapter, every path that leads to glory contains a unique storm, a storm that creates obstacles that an individual can only conquer by fighting.

All life is beautiful, so it makes sense that to live a life of satisfaction fully requires a fight as hard and fair as life itself.

Even the Bible intertwines fighting for what we believe to be best and insists we fight the good fight of faith. Jesus fought this very fight, starting from his persecution, to his crucifixion, to his resurrection.

Why Should We Fight?

The battles of life that we endure are the very foundations needed to determine the level of fight necessary to overcome our obstacles.

Poverty is a perfect example of an obstacle that must be overcome to ensure personal safety and overall happiness. If you do not fight to rise above the oppressive nature of poverty, long-term survival is not guaranteed. Most children born into a home in Africa will experience, from the very first breath they take, a war-torn environment. There is no wonder why most African parents begin a quest of true spirituality after visiting a seer to determine their new baby's future and what it holds.

Ask an MD or GMD about the struggles they have endured over the years, and they can tell you the effort it took to get into the current position they hold. Speak to them about their travail, the attacks they experienced, and all the dark moments that shadowed their pasts, and you learn that it took an unimaginable level of fight and will to triumph.

I can speak from authentic experience on the matter of fighting to survive. Growing up, I came face to face with several challenges. I have suffered memory loss, battled a tumour and won, and experienced chronic headaches. My health issues occurred when I was a child, and I learned earlier than most, that the key to life is never to give up the fight. If I had given up my on my faith and myself, I would not be here to tell my story. As noted by Isah Blessing, "We will always have to struggle, we are meant to continue fighting, let us say to ourselves we will win."

Life is about happiness and fulfillment, and doing good for others, but life is also about how much you will fight to survive the bad times.

As Maria Odoh states, "Life is about how [many] steps you can take and keep fighting.

Also, how much you can suffer and keep." Barriers, chains, infirmity, and afflictions won't break unless we break them with a fight.

About the initial question, why should we keep fighting? Here are a few reasons as highlighted in the text above.

1. To meet the needs of life.

2. To overcome the obstacles of life.

3. To occupy your place of destiny (Prayer)

4. To win specific critical issues of life (Prayer)

1. To Meet the needs of life

Every fight in life demands a specific reason before a person can commit to engaging in battle. One reason a person may commit to a conflict is to meet the needs necessary to ensure survival.

In our everyday life, we see people waking up and working or doing whatever they need to so that their basic needs are met. There is not a single person living who would starve to death over enjoying the fruits of their labour. The saying, "No work, no pay," means what it says. If we do not purposely seek employment to fight for our own needs, who will? We cannot expect the heavens to open up and rain down upon us the very essentials needed to live. You are responsible for your own needs and cannot rely on others to meet your needs.

An important thing to remember, and is often easy to forget, is just because you cannot meet your needs; today, it does not mean that life will always be that way. Through the fight, your current status, background, and conditions can be changed.

As you mature through life, you realise that your current situations are not set in stone. Doing without today does not mean you will do without forever. If you want to improve your conditions, fight!

Every single day you fight is a day closer to changing what is making you unhappy and leading you to a better life. Your current situation is temporary. Your background is behind you. All that matters is where you direct yourself tomorrow. The best way to lead is by fighting for the tomorrow that you want to create.

2. To overcome the obstacles of life.

The Bible's book of Ephesians makes it clear for us we are not contending against flesh and blood, but against the principalities, against the powers, against the world rulers of this present generation, and the spiritual hosts of wickedness in the heavenly places.

Think of life as a peaceful field of wildflowers being destroyed by evildoers. To keep the field of wildflowers around for future generations to enjoy, we must fight the evildoers and prevent them from killing the natural beauty before us.

Warfare is a villain that many around the world are still coming up against. We have seen movies that use war as a means of entertainment, but videos cannot capture the actual fear, devastation, and depression caused by the constant fighting. Battles, as discussed previously, cannot be won with arsenals of weaponry, but through prayer, praise, and sacrifice of the innocent bystanders unwillingly standing between enemy lines.

3. To occupy your place of destiny (Prayer).

As noted in 2 Corinthians 10:4 (RSV), "for the weapons of our warfare are not worldly but have divine power to destroy strongholds." For this argument, I will define prayer as an act of communication between two realms, the natural realm, and the supernatural realm.

While in prayer, exchanges are happening, and a transaction of a different kind is taking place. Prayer is powerful ammunition for breaking chains, barriers, and seeing through dark clouds. We can never improve our conditions without harnessing the power of fear. Prayer is even practiced by the herbalist who uses prayer as his incantations. Prayer is a mystery that governs the unseen. You can't see it but can feel the power of its answers. Prayer is evidence that you are fighting for the best livelihood possible, a stronghold of your existence against the forces trying to ruin your desired way of life.

When you pray, your wishes are made known before the head of the realm you're consulting. It could be the realm of Jesus, or Buddha, perhaps that of Mohammed, or even Ogun.

In various offices today, you will notice battles and signs of the fight, both spiritually and physically. Take the time to observe someone in a management position. If you think a person isn't facing competition from internal and external conflict, and others willing to do whatever it takes to take over that person's job, you are wrong.

You must keep fighting on, praying fervently, having the mind-set of Priscilla Shirer, the heroine of the award-winning gospel movie "War Room," and also understanding the secrets kept locked in the preverbal closet.

As a civil servant, student, banker, engineer, or doctor, you must pray, because the Devil will do anything in his power to interfere with not only your happiness but also your destiny. I urge you to take the time to pray, as I cannot stress how beneficial it is.

Just as the herbalist gets strength through the recitation of his incantations, we strengthen our minds and our souls whenever we pray.

Prayer to a higher power feeds the spirit of man and repels him from temptation. As Jesus stated to the apostles in Matthew 26:41, "watch and pray that you don't fall into temptation; the spirit is willing, but the flesh is weak."

I firmly believe and affirm that life's most critical issues can only be solved by opening a line of communication between man and God. Consider the great minds that have walked this earth; Einstein was just one genius that has contributed to science. Even with these great minds, scientists could not cure all deadly diseases and infections. Tuberculosis has plagued the world with no cure for centuries. HIV and other sexually transmitted infections continue to spread with no known cure in sight. If it were possible to cure these diseases with pure human intellect, do you think they would still be a problem with all the modern advancements and technologies we have to date? No, because prayer is the only cure for such travesties.

Pray like Daniel, fight like David, and never stopped giving up, until you reach your expectation like Hannah.

Summary

Prayer is a network connecting the individual with a different realm.

Not all critical cases can be solved with human intellect, but with prayer.

We fight, occupy, and triumph through prayer.

Courage

“No one has ever stared the possibility of a devastating battle in the eyes without mustering up true courage to be victorious.” - Stephen Edoh.

Imagine walking into the home of a friend for the first time, only to be confronted with the angry growl of a German Shepherd. Your human instinct is to run, and I imagine that’s what most people would do.

In life, when we come face-to-face with an unexpected obstacle (a metaphorical German Shepherd), we cannot run and hide. We can only continue to walk the road ahead by holding our heads high and letting courage guide our way.

Courage causes a surge in our adrenal gland and gives us the energy we need to carry on and fight our battles.

In every negative situation you find yourself in, remember that circumstances are just temporary and that sometimes the terrible experiences are part of getting to the ideal outcome. You were not born to live in a constant state of despair.

Face every unusual situation with courage, don't be like the spies, who were sent to examine the Promise Land, as reviewed by the Bible. However, be the Joshua of your day and have the Caleb mind-set in you.

No matter how down you may be, never engage in any pessimistic attitude or try to drag others down with you. A man of courage cannot achieve success with a negative mindset. Surround yourself with those who fill you with positivity and be the same person to them.

Remember, courage does not demand a person to be rich, famous, or well respected. No matter what the person's income or situation, anybody can find courage from within. As said by Napoleon Hill, "If you cannot do great things, do small things greatly." If you cannot find the courage within, fake it.

Every stage in life requires a great fight. Courage is needed at every step to continue to be victorious on the battlefield of life.

Remember friends, keep the courage up, because to have it going altitudinous, it pays.

Summary

Every life carrier organism must fight to triumph.

Prayer is the only factor that can only secure your destiny.

Courage is adrenaline, get it from your adrenal gland.

Victory in life comes as a result of continuous fight, courage, and prayer — Stephen Edoh.

To support Stephen Edoh's ministries, kindly forward your assistance to the PayPal address below:

PayPal: stephenedoh2000@gmail.com

PayPal.me/Stephenedoh

Four

The travails

The condition that year wasn't a good one, it's created an unstable moment for everyone, especially labourers who then act arduous. The magnitude to which one endure and triumph over certain things in life is indeed a great one. Understanding time and seasons must be reasoned through the great travail. While in the storm, you have to keep fighting to prevail in the travail. The travail is a series in life. There comes a time in life, we need to be exposed to a dimension we aren't acquainted with.

Jesus Christ endured the travail, he pushed through the struggle, he went through an ache situation and at the end, he prevailed over the travail. Suffering is a mystery that makes us understand the value of certain things in life, it's prepared us for the future task, also mature our spirit mind.

The Eiffel tower is beautiful, but it takes a lot of energy, time, effort and of patients to get it built. Try researching on the chronicle of Eiffel tower, you will know how much the workers then, suffered.

What if Sir Eiffel has given up on his plan? Paris today, wouldn't have any top attractive monument, a charming tourist from different part of the world. But thank God he never gave up.

Striking and striving are continuous processes in life. We keep working hard every day for the aim of survival. The struggle of life isn't a beautiful one, the fruit is.

The struggles you faced aren't your enemy, they are your lifting up strategies. Always have it in mind, that you must do what you have never done, to get you what you have never got before.

Claiming victory in the travail is the sweetest mystery anybody will ever experience. It takes patience and time to achieve this.

Walking in the dark phase

Have you ever walked through a dark path ?? Yes, of course, will be your answer. I know while walking in that phase, you weren't comfortable, you felt dismayed until you find the light.

So many times in our struggle, we forget certain things. We forget where we started from, and of all, most people don't think of where they are going to, rather than their present state. We must always endure, tolerate and struggle through any condition we found ourselves, no matter the hardship we faced.

The hardship we faced in life is like ingredients used in preparing a stew. We all know, a stew is sweet, and it's of gorgeous delicacy.

Remember earlier I said, every path to glory need a fight and must be reasoned through the travail. The stew of life demand more to be prepared, taste and consumed.

You want something good, work for it. You need something beautiful, fight for it. You aim for something flamboyant, then strike hard, pray hard and play hard to get it –Edoh Stephen.

The dark phase isn't the ugly situation we found ourselves, but the ignorance that kept us in that ugly situation — Edoh Stephen

How do you feel after walking all day, and your efforts end up being fruitless? oh, I feel anguish, I understand the agony you went through, but know this beloved it is only for a moment.

Beloved always remember in the struggle, there is someone who was in the past, who is there now and will still be there in the future. He is the light in the dark, the lily of the valley, the water in the desert, the hope in storm, the one who gives tranquillity, in him we found all this, Jesus.

You couldn't afford two per meal yesterday, but today you do. Never give up, a time is coming you will become feeders of nations.

Conquering the dark path must be an embraced challenge, that must be faced with courage.

Tracing back to history, you will agree with me, some notorious people especially freedom fighters, heroes of faith and human activist's fought through the Travail and came out victorious, only by their ability to be patient and cool tracked with time.

Let's find out about those who fought the war indeed the great travail and came out victorious. I called them "The Magnificent"

NELSON MANDELA

Black isn't beautiful if you forget talking about the struggle, the pain, the persistence, the courage and victory of Nelson Madiba Mandela.

Indeed, the talk of freedom was an irony for every Africa nation until the late 50s.

The young man Nelson Mandela was someone beyond a freedom fighter, but indeed a pain the colonial Masters couldn't bear in their nerves.

Mandela was born on 18 July 1918 in the village of

Mvezo in Umtata , then part of South Africa's Cape Province. Given the forename Rolihlahla, a Xhosa term colloquially meaning "troublemaker", in later years he became known by his clan name,

Madiba. His patrimonial great-grandfather, Ngubengcuka , was king of the Thembu people in the Transkeian Territories of South Africa's modern Eastern Cape province.

He grew up with two sisters in his mother's kraal in the village of Qunu , where he tended herds as a cattle-boy and spent much time outside with other boys. Both his parents were illiterate, but being a devout Christian, his mother sent him to a local Methodist school when he was about seven. Baptized a Methodist, Mandela was given the English forename of "Nelson" by his teacher.

When Mandela was about nine, his father came to stay at Qunu, where he died of an undiagnosed ailment which Mandela believed to be lung disease. Feeling "cut adrift", he later said that he inherited his father's "proud rebelliousness" and "stubborn sense of fairness."

In 1933 Mandela began his secondary education at Clarkebury Methodist High School in Engcobo , a Western-style institution that was the largest school for black Africans in Thembuland. Made to socialize with other students on an equal basis, he claimed that he lost his "stuck up" attitude, becoming best friends with a girl for the first time; he began playing sports and developed his lifelong love of gardening.

He completed his Junior Certificate in two years, and in 1937 moved to Healdtown , the Methodist college in Fort Beaufort attended by most Thembu royalty, including Justice.

The headmaster emphasized the superiority of English culture and government, but Mandela became increasingly interested in native African culture, making his first non-Xhosa friend, a speaker of Sotho , and coming under the influence of one of his favourite teachers, a Xhosa who broke a taboo by marrying a Sotho.

Mandela spent much of his spare time at Healdtown as a long-distance runner and boxer, and in his second year, he became perfect.

In 1939 Mandela began work on a BA degree at the University of Fort Hare, an elite black institution in Alice, Eastern Cape, with around 150 students. There he studied English, anthropology, politics, native administration, and Roman-Dutch law in his first year, desiring to become an interpreter or clerk in the Native Affairs Department.

Mandela stayed in the Wesley House dormitory, befriending his own kinsman, K. D. Matanzima, as well as Oliver Tambo, who became a close friend and comrade for decades to come. He took up ballroom dancing, performed in a drama society play about Abraham Lincoln, and gave Bible classes in the local community as part of the Student Christian Association.

Although he had friends connected to the African

National Congress (ANC) who wanted South

Africa to be independent of the British Empire,

Mandela avoided any involvement with the antiimperialist movement and became a vocal supporter of the British war effort when the Second World War broke out.

He helped to found a first-year students' house committee which challenged the dominance of the second-years, and at the end of his first year became involved in a Students' Representative Council (SRC) boycott against the quality of food, for which he was suspended from the university; he never returned to complete his degree. In 1941, aged 23, he ran away from an arranged marriage and went to Johannesburg.

Two years later, he enrolled for a law degree at the mainly white Witswaterand University, where he met people from all races and backgrounds. He was exposed to liberal, radical and Africanist thought, as well as racism and discrimination, which fuelled his passion for politics.

The same year, he joined the African National Congress (ANC) and later co-founded the ANC Youth League.

He married his first wife, Evelyn Mase, in 1944.

They got divorced after having four children.

Mr. Mandela qualified as a lawyer and in 1952 opened a law practice in Johannesburg with his partner, Oliver Tambo.

Together, Mr. Mandela and Mr. Tambo campaigned against

apartheid, the system devised by the all-white National Party which oppressed the black majority.

In 1956, Mr. Mandela was charged with high treason, along with 155 other activists, but the charges against him were dropped after a four-year trial.

Resistance to apartheid grew, mainly against the new Pass Laws, which dictated where black people were allowed to live and work.

In 1958, Mr. Mandela married Winnie Madikizela, who was later to take an active role in the campaign to free her husband from prison.

The ANC was outlawed in 1960 and Mr. Mandela went underground.

Tension with the apartheid regime grew and soared to new heights in 1960 when 69 black people were shot dead by police in the Sharpeville massacre.

Life sentence!

This marked the end of peaceful resistance and Mr. Mandela, already national vice-president of the ANC launched a campaign of economic sabotage.

He was eventually arrested and charged with sabotage and attempting to violently overthrow the government.

Speaking from the dock in the Rivonia court room, Mr. Mandela used the stand to convey his beliefs about democracy, freedom, and equality.

"I have cherished the ideal of a democratic and free society in which all persons will live together in harmony and with equal opportunities," he said. "It is an ideal for which I hope to live for and to see realized. But if needs be, it is an ideal for which I am prepared to die."

In the winter of 1964, he was sentenced to life in prison.

In the space of 12 months between 1968 and 1969, Mr. Mandela's mother died and his eldest son was killed in a car crash, but he was not allowed to attend the funerals.

He remained in prison on Robben Island for 18 years before being transferred to Pollsmoor Prison on the mainland in 1982.

As Mr. Mandela and other ANC leaders languished in prison or lived in exile, the youths of South Africa's black townships did their best to fight white minority rule.

Hundreds were killed, and thousands were injured before the schoolchildren's uprising was crushed.

In 1980, the ANC led by the exiled Mr. Tambo, launched an international campaign against apartheid but ingeniously decided to focus it on one cause and one person — the demand to release Mr. Mandela.

This culminated in 1988 concert at the stadium in London when some 72,000 people — and millions more watching on TV around the world — sang "Free Nelson Mandela."

Popular pressure led world leaders to tighten the sanctions first imposed on South Africa in 1967 against the apartheid regime.

The pressure produced results, and in 1990, President FW de Klerk lifted the ban on the ANC. Mr. Mandela was released from prison and talks on forming a new multi-racial democracy for South Africa began.

Having read line by line the struggles Nelson Mandela went through, you will agree with me, this man was fearless, patience, also a man who loved the people and of all, a man who never give up.

Life is full of travail. You must learn to keep strong, while the odds get better. Madiba never gave up, he kept saying this to himself and the other detainees, " Our walk to freedom will prevail " and at the end of travail, they prevailed.

Do you ever imagine how long, he kept waiting for his freedom and that of his people ??

Think of the treatment he received while in prison, think of the depression and regret he might once have thought of...

What were the reactions of South Africans, after he was sent to prison, No hope again ??

Beloved don't panic, while you're in the travail.

Isaiah 53:11 made it clear to us that " He shall see the fruit of his travail and be satisfied " so understand that at the end of the pain, you shall go celebrating joyously.

HANNAH

Ask an African woman who has been married for years without a child, then hear her response. Imagine the pressure being mounted on her by her in-laws, the insult she has received so far, the shame of barrenness.

Do you think a farmer will be happy, after the trees he planted after so many years remain barren, even when their time has come to bear fruit ?? Not at all.

There lived a woman called Hannah in the Biblical

City of Ephraim. She lives with her husband Elkanah and his wife Penninah, she was barren for years.

Hannah was loved by Elkanah. He Elkanah goes to Shiloh every year before the Lord to offer sacrifice.

It's quite unfortunate, God himself closed the womb of Hannah.

But he did it for the purpose of passing a message to the future generations and here we come to be witnesses.

Hannah was one who went through pain in her husband house. One who was mocked, insulted, I feel bad for Hannah. But she never gave up, even though she was distressed and depressed.

Hannah prays, she knows her situation wasn't shouting around nor activating a mood of jealousy within her. But indeed she went to her secret place and source out the answer to her agony.

Up to a point, Eli the priest couldn't contain the waves of anguish passing the temple, he knows the woman was in vain, a woman in the worst of her moment.

Sometimes we must learn from others to know how better, the go goes in the travail.

What if Hannah has complained and not take any action ?? oh! the case will still be the same.

But she was patient, and she ends up in her joyous home like the psalmist quoted in Psalm:19 " He gives the barren woman a home, making her the joyous mother of children. Praise the Lord!

Hannah was futile, fruitless, ineffectual but God changed her story to glory, in the end, she, bored sons and daughters.

Praise God!

J.K. ROWLING'S

Happiness is a factor that will make one feel calm, joyous and relaxed.

One of the evidence of happiness can be found in movies.

Without J. K Rowling's impact, I strongly believe that Hollywood wouldn't be complete in every dimension. When we speak of movie genres. Creating her book series wasn't as easy as scribbling down the note on a few dinner napkins. It wasn't a one, two or even three step process. It would take years of perseverance to become the success she is today.

Soon after conceiving the idea for Harry Potter, Rowling began writing but was immediately pulled away from her work by the devastating death of her mother. Rowling ceased working on the book and sank into a deep, grieving depression, getting little to nothing accomplished in that time.

In the hopes of digging herself out of grievance, she took a job teaching English in Portugal for a year. Her goal in venturing abroad was to get away from her troubles and more importantly, use her time off to continue working on her book. She set the goal of having the first Harry Potter book done by the time she returned from Portugal.

Things did not go as planned.

Not only did she fail to make progress on her first book, but after falling in, and then out of, love, she ended up with a failed marriage and a baby daughter she now had to raise alone. She came back to nothing.

She had no job, no finished product and two mouths to feed. She had hit rock bottom.

As she struggled with depression, raising a child on her own and living off meagre unemployment benefits, she resumed work on her book in cafes while her daughter was asleep.

Despite numerous setbacks, she found solace in doing what she loved – writing. In fact, she found that the little she had were enough to be moderately happy. She had ended up in exactly the position she had feared most and found that it wasn't that bad. There wasn't anything left to be afraid of and her work showcased that mind-set. When Rowling finally finished the first three chapters, she sent the manuscript off to a publisher — They quickly passed on the project.

She sent it to another publisher. Again, the answer was no. Her mailbox filled up with rejection letters, but she didn't let it stop her.

"Failure meant a stripping away of the inessential. I stopped pretending to myself that I was anything other than what I was, and began to direct all my energy into finishing the only work that mattered to me."
—- J.K. Rowling

After sending her manuscript to 12 different publishers and getting rejected by every single one, Rowling began losing confidence in her book. Finally, the editor at Bloomsbury Publishing company sat down to read the manuscript and so did the editor's 8-year-old daughter.

The little girl loved the opening chapters and begged to read the whole thing. This made the publisher agree to publish Rowling's novel.

But Rowling was left with a warning: that she should get a day job because she wouldn't make any money writing children's books. Once Harry Potter and the Sorcerer's Stone was published, though, she proved everyone wrong.

J.K. Rowling went from being a jobless single mother living off unemployment benefits to one of the best-selling authors of all-time.

But it didn't happen overnight. She faced rejection and constantly strove for success. She worked hard at her craft before anyone noticed her.

That practice, along with strengthening herself against rejection, was what made her work unforgettable.

Looking back, the Harry Potter series has earned over $400 million in book sales, and the last movie alone earned $476 million dollars in ticket sales on opening weekend. She was the first female to become a billionaire author, not that many authors make it that far in the first place.

If you have a dream or a passion and you keep getting rejected or running into failure, don't let that stop you. If you're going through a tough time in your life, but working on something you really believe in, don't give up. If you do, you'll never know what could have been. Who knows, you might end up breaking records.

The bittersweet story of J.K. Rowling went from grass to grace, zero to hero, poverty to prosperity, only due to the fact that she embraced perseverance and patience.

Just being rejected by five publishers is enough to let you know that, you have not done well. But J.K.

Rowling didn't give up, she fought hard in the travail and came out victorious.

Keep strong!!

OPRAH WINFREY.

Setbacks, assault, pains aren't there to kill you, but to be your lifting up strategies-Stephen Edoh

In life, you will come across different people, walk through different roads, encounter different situations, but in time we overcome all these.

For many decades, Oprah Winfrey has made the black race proud.

She was such an influencing woman, a darling worth applauding, a genius and a heroine of our time.

Born to a single teenage mother on welfare in rural Mississippi. She felt unwanted and was shuttled back and forth from her grandmother to her mother, and then to her father by the time she was 14.

She lived in poverty and suffered abuse for years. This does not sound like the beginnings of a media mogul who would go on to own a cable network and become one of America's most influential people and the first African-American billionaire, and yet it is.

A Childhood of Abuse.

In fact, Oprah had to overcome many challenges and obstacles before achieving the success she enjoys today.

She began life on a small farm in Mississippi where her strict grandmother raised her. "I was beaten regularly," she told David Letterman during a lecture series at Ball State University.

She recalled a time that her grandmother punished her for putting her fingers in a bucket of water she had retrieved from the well. "She whipped me so badly that I had welts on my back and the welts would bleed," she said, which then stained her good Sunday dress. "So then I got another whipping for getting blood on the dress." She was also lonely much of the time and due to her family's poverty, conditions were poor. But her grandmother taught her to read before she was three years old, and she still recalls the positive reception she received when she recited Bible verses at her grandmother's church.

The sense of approval and acceptance she felt after speaking to the congregation stayed with her and influenced her future career choices.

At six years old, Oprah went to live with her mother in Milwaukee, Wisconsin. Since her mother worked long hours as a maid, Oprah was neglected. At nine years old, she was left in the care of her 19-year-old cousin who had raped her. She continued to suffer sexual abuse from other relatives, including her mother's boyfriend until she was 13yers old when she ran away from home. At 14, she became pregnant (the baby died shortly after birth) and she moved in with her father in Tennessee.

Rescued by Education.

Oprah's father made education a high priority for Oprah. "My father turned my life around by insisting that I be more than I was," Oprah said in an interview. "His love of learning showed me the way." She began attending Nashville East High School where she took public speaking and drama and was even elected school president.

She received a full scholarship to Tennessee State

University after winning a public speaking contest. She had a few broadcasting jobs before being named the talk show host for a morning show called People Are Talking.

From there her rising career is well-known—she took a job as host of A.M. Chicago, which became the highest-rated talk show in Chicago and was renamed The Oprah Winfrey Show.

Learning from her Painful Past.

"The human experience of yours is stunning,"

David Letterman told Oprah during the Ball State University interview. "I am so grateful for my years literally living in poverty," she replied, "because it makes the experience of creating success and building success that much more rewarding."

Oprah has continued to build on her own success; she created a monthly magazine, O, The Oprah

Magazine, has produced a variety of films, syndicated television programs, and a Broadway musical, and was nominated for Best Supporting Actress for her role in The Colour Purple.

In 2011, she launched her own cable network,

OWN. Time.com and CNN have called her the "world's most powerful woman" and she has appeared on Time's "100 most influential" list ten times since 2004, the only person to have appeared on the list that many times.

And from 2004 until 2010, she was ranked among the "50 most generous Americans," giving away nearly $400 million to educational causes. Oprah developed a number of character traits as a result of living through these childhood traumas, many of which she now attributes to her success. "My story just helped define and shape me as does everybody's story,"

The fact raped she was raped in her teens, didn't stop her from achieving her dreams, the fact she was neglected didn't bring her down, she kept pressing hard, aiming towards a glorious future and today she's the most influencing woman in our generation.

Don't give up, you can be the Oprah Winfrey of your time, keep strong and soar!

MAHATMA GANDHI

Nothing is as sweet as freedom-Stephen Edoh

Some have fought for the sake of survival, others for land, money, etc. But the real men actually fought for freedom.

Freedom is never given, it's won.

Men like Mahatma Gandhi made a great impact in inspiring future generations to keep fighting for freedom.

Mohandas Mahatma Gandhi was born in the western part of British-ruled India on October 2, 1869.

A timid child, he was married at thirteen to a girl of the same age, Kasturba.

Following the death of his father, Gandhi's family sent him to England in 1888 to study law. There, he became interested in the philosophy of nonviolence, as expressed in the Bhagavad-Gita, Hindu sacred scripture, and in Jesus Christ's Sermon on the Mount in the Christian Bible.

He returned to India in 1891, having passed the bar, but found little success in his attempts to practice law. Seeking a change of scenery, he accepted a position in South Africa for a year, where he assisted on a lawsuit.

In South Africa, he became involved in efforts to end discrimination against the Indian minority there, who were oppressed both by the

British and by the Boers, descendants of the original Dutch settlers of the region.

Having intended to stay a year, he ended up remaining until 1914 (his wife and children had joined him, meanwhile, in 1896). He founded the Natal Indian Congress, which worked to further Indian interests, and commanded an Indian medical corps that fought on the British side in the Boer War (1899-1901), in which the British conquered the last independent Boer republics.

After the war, Gandhi reputation as a leader grew. He became even more adamant in his personal principles, practicing sexual abstinence, renouncing modern technology, and developing satyagraha–literally, "soul- force." Satyagraha was a method of non-violent resistance, often called "non-cooperation," that he and his allies used to great effect against the white governments in South Africa.

Their willingness to endure punishment and jail earned the admiration of people in Gandhi's native India and eventually won concessions from the Boer and British rulers.

By 1914, when Gandhi left South Africa and returned to India, he was known as a holy man: people called him a "Mahatma", or "great soul."

At this point, he was still loyal to the British

Empire, but when the British cracked down on Indian civil liberties after World War I, Gandhi began to organize nonviolent protests.

The Amritsar Massacre, in which British troops gunned down peaceful Indian protesters, convinced Gandhi and India of the need for self-rule, and in the early '20s, Gandhi organized large-scale campaigns of non-cooperation that paralyzed the subcontinent's administration–and led to his imprisonment, from 1922 to 1924.

After his release, he withdrew from politics for a time, preferring to travel India, working among the peasantry. But in 1930, he wrote the Declaration of Independence of India and then led the Salt March in protest against the British monopoly on salt.

This touched off acts of civil disobedience across India, and the British were forced to invite Gandhi to London for a Round-Table Conference.

Although Gandhi received a warm welcome in England, the Conference foundered on the issue of how an independent India would deal with its Muslim minority, and Gandhi withdrew from public life again. But independence could not be long delayed.

The Government of India Act (1935) surrendered significant amounts of power to Indians, and the Indian National Congress clamoured for more. When World War II broke out, India erupted into violence, and many nationalist leaders, including Gandhi, went to prison.

After the war, the new British government wanted to get India off its hands quickly. But Muhammed Ali Jinnah, the head of the Muslim League, demanded that a separate state be created for India's Muslims, and to Gandhi's great distress, the Congress leaders and the harried British agreed. August 1947 saw India's attainment of independence–as well as its partition into two countries, India and Pakistan.

However, neither measure served to solve India's problems, and the country immediately fell apart:

Hindus and Muslims killed each other in alarming numbers while refugees fled toward the borders. Heartbroken, Gandhi tried to calm the country, but to no avail.

He was assassinated by a Hindu nationalist in Delhi on January 30, 1948, and India mourned the loss of its greatest hero.

Life in the travail is about one capacity to be patience and calm.

Giving up isn't the best thing to do when you are in pain, indeed rise, speak to yourself these words, I will leave this situation soon.

Summary

In life, we must learn to struggle, fight and keep calm.

Freedom and joy are the rewards of patience in the travail.

Assault, racism, rape, etc. can't stop you from achieving your dream, they are only there to make you strong.

II

The phase of restructuring

Five

Times and seasons

Physicists have made it known to us that everything on earth act regarding time.

Time is an inevitable progression into the future with the passing of present events into the past. The basic concepts of success are governed and manipulated by time. Every individual must understand the value of time, the effects of time and the consequences that will be faced when time is misused.

In our everyday life, we experience a natural phenomenon of going to bed at night and waking up at day. These simple facts describe the mystery of time.

The high level of knowledge must coordinate your journey to a new dawn you have concerning time. The difference between a mediocre and an optimist is their value for time- Stephen Edoh.

There is this famous saying "time spent rightly is gain, time spent wrongly is loss ". Learning to invest positively in time is a pertinent idea leading one to success. You must learn to invest well in time. It is the same thing as investing in an excellent woman, only to end up having a pleasant home.

The bible clarified that there is a time for everything.

Eccl 3:1-8

There is a time for everything, and a season for every activity under heaven:

A time to be born and a time to die,

A time to plant and a time to uproot,

A time to kill and a time to heal,

A time to tear down and a time to build,

A time to weep and a time to laugh,

A time to mourn and a time to dance,

A time to scatter stones and a time to gather stones

A time to embrace and a time to refrain,

A time to search and a time to give up,

A time to keep and a time to throw away,

A time to tear and a time to mend,

A time to be silent and a time to speak,

A time to love and a time to hate,

A time for war and a time for peace.

Learn how to use the right time for the right thing. Don't use the time for sowing for another thing, otherwise you will have nothing to harvest during the harvest season. Be at the right place at the right time. Always be on time.

Never allow yourself to be found in the company of peoples who dis valued time.

An understanding of time and seasons will bring an end to fear, anxiety and every problem.

UNDERSTANDING TIME AND SEASONS

In understanding time and seasons, a certain principle must be followed.

Punctuality and Self-discipline have proven to be an effective tool in time management. Time and seasons are instruments of measurement, assessment, planning, and perfection.

Time is an effective tool in the hands of God in planning and executing his plans. In time, everything that has a beginning must have an end. When you learn to be sensitive to the use of time, you realise, it's not only profit for you but gives you more space to accomplish some other tasks.

What makes a man difference and effectual is his ability to understand, control, and manage time. Your vision, dreams, ambition, desires and all of your wishes become a reality when there is a proper understanding of time.

Every season in life is pregnant with accolades, ideas, inspirations, harvest, joy, etc. like the farmer who plants at springtime and harvest his crop during the season of harvest. Our lives should be as that of the farmer concerning the planting of crops and harvest.

The planting season here shows the period you invest, the period you sacrifice, that moment where you toil. While the season of harvest is that in which you glow in joy, your investment in time and the sacrifices you made in your travail.

The previous chapters were mainly concerned with the teaching, coaching and nurturing of one into a new dawn. The same goes with this chapter.

Time is one of the basic tools in describing the path of a new dawn. The moment of pain, joy, and happiness all walked through time.

For you to understand time and seasons, the tips below can be of great help.

*Punctuality✓

*Self Discipline✓

*Wisdom✓

PUNCTUALITY

Punctuality is the act of being able to complete a required task or fulfil an obligation before or at a previously designated time.

Often people failed to comply with the fact of being punctual. Go to office today. You will find out how most public servants battle to be punctual.

You can't be the best if you aren't punctual.

An individual whose life is not punctual becomes a breeding ground for failure.

When one learns to cultivate the habit of punctuality, it's become a character of success leading to a culture of greatness. Punctuality is that which step you up, while you embark on your journey to greatness before any other key factor comes in.

Without punctuality, man can't fulfil most of his purposes.

I will wake up very early in the morning, to prepare for the day, not forgetting to fasten my

belt also has it clear to me "I will always win "–Stephen Edoh

Waking up very early brings a lot of motivation because it incites you to accomplish every task so fast and gives you room to be free for a while.

The best student in every class pays the price of being punctual with their book to be at the level of effulgence.

(HOW TO BE PUNCTUAL)

* Learn to be conscious of time.

* Always be ready to get a task done.

* Adopt a winning mind-set.* Always go to bed on time.

(BENEFIT OF PUNCTUALITY)

* Dreams become reality when one is punctual.

* It creates a unique and acceptable view in an individual.

* Punctuality helps accomplished our day-to-day activities within a short time.

SELF DISCIPLINE

Self-discipline is the ability to do the expected of you as a certain period.

Without self-discipline, you walk to a new dawn will never be a reality.

Successful people are disciplined people. They take control of their wants, feelings, and thoughts, which affect what they say and do.

"Self-discipline is the key to personal greatness. With self-discipline, the average person can rise as far and as fast as his talents and intelligence can take him. But without self-discipline, a person with every blessing of background, education, and opportunity will seldom rise above mediocrity." - Brian Tracey.

Just as self discipline is the key to greatness and success, also lack of self-discipline is the major cause of failure, frustration, underachievement, and unhappiness in life. There is perhaps no area of your life in which self-discipline is more important than in the way you manage your time. Time is a special resource that you cannot store or save for later use.

Everyone has the same time each day. We cannot recover time not well used. The fact is that you cannot save time; you can only spend it differently. You can only reallocate your time usage from areas of low value to areas of chief value.

Have you ever noticed that the things that matter most often get pushed aside by less important concerns? You would be very upset if someone gained access to your bank account and stole all your money.

Most people, though, don't blink an eye when many culprits sneak into their lives and steal their time.

Below is the list of things that consumed our time;

* Gossiping

* Procrastination

* unnecessary hangout

* Too much play

° You must avoid gossiping to create time for positive thoughts and aspiration.

° Procrastination is a killer and an enemy of progress. You must ensure you run a task as fast as you can.

° Spending too much time with friends isn't advisable. Sometimes you have to be alone to plan.

° It's good when you find time playing, but not when the "too "comes in. You will find out that when you gave so much time to play, you become less productive.

Our lives must embrace self-discipline to understand seasons and advance to a new dawn.

(BENEFIT OF SELF DISCIPLINE)

* Self-discipline makes one a better time manager.

* Self-discipline build excellent reputation in the life of an individual.

* Self-discipline gains an individual admiration from others.

WISDOM

Happy is the man who finds wisdom, and the

Man who gets understanding. proverb 3:13

RSV

Wisdom is the ability to apply relevant knowledge insightfully, especially to different situations from that in which the knowledge was gained.

Without wisdom, you won't cross certain boundaries in life, but end up quarter way in your journey to a new dawn.

Time and seasons will always work out in favour of those who operate in the wisdom dimension-Stephen Edoh

The major key factor used in discovering the hidden treasures of life is wisdom.

Wisdom plays a dominant role in the life of an individual who perseveres. It is wisdom that makes one senses a situation and believe no situation is permanent.

In life, you must adopt wisdom as your soulmate.

Find time reading, researching, learning, sporting, etc, but remember never to spend all your time in these activities.

You find time getting better as an individual with a difference, when you walked in the wisdom pathway.

Getting wisdom is pivotal and relevant to understanding times and seasons.

Let us look at a few points that could expand our wisdom dimensions in understanding time and seasons;

* The Renewal of the mind✓

* Learning new things✓

* Adopting an optimism spirit✓

• The Renewal of the mind

* Our mind is the centre focal point of our life, where several psychological activities take place.

* Our thoughts give rise to the feelings we have towards certain thing's, to the words we speak, and also to our actions.

* We must learn to change our thoughts and place our mind on positive things.

* The wisdom dimension of our life expands when there is a complete renewal of the mind. * You will never understand the time in your hand and the seasons in your life if you refused to renew your mind.

When your mind is renewed, you experienced a change in your life, your level of understanding change, your thought change, and also your words change.

Do not be conformed to this world but be transformed by the renewal of your mind, that you may prove what is the will of God, what is acceptable and perfect. Rom 12:2

RSV

• Learning new things

I will define learning, as the acts of acquiring knowledge.

In life we keep learning daily, gaining more experience from past occurrences, also using these experiences to solve problems.

It's hard to gain wisdom when you stay indoors and do the same thing day after day. You get wiser when you put yourself out there and give yourself the opportunity to learn, make mistakes and reflect on the experience.

Every time you experience something new, you open yourself up to the possibility of learning and getting a little wiser for having tried it.

The seasons of life are being conquered by those who spend more time learning, trying out something new.

While you keep learning new things, you become competent and extraordinary in understanding times and seasons.

• Adopting an optimistic spirit

* Results gotten in time and seasons are clearly based on optimism or pessimism. * An optimist rules times and seasons. * What differentiates an optimist from a mediocre is level of understanding concerning time and seasons the optimist has. * A mediocre life and walks in the path of indifference, nonchalance, and carelessness. Never hang out with pessimists, because you aren't a mediocre, else if you do, you then be like them.

Your journey to a new dawn is being fast-tracked, when you adopt the mind-set of an optimist. An individual who aims higher will never fear facing obstacles, challenges, and battles of life.

When you adopt the spirit of optimism, you experience victory, breakthrough, and success in all areas of your life. As you keep renewing your mind, learning new things and living an optimist life; You'll come to understand the wisdom dimensions to rule in times and seasons.

The benefit of understanding time and seasons.

1. An understanding of time and seasons will bring rest and destroy fear concerning the problems of life.

2. It will build patience in you because you will do everything that has a beginning must have an end.

3. It will help you prepare for the next season of your life.

4 It will help you take advantage of the time and seasons of your life and ride in the momentum that it creates.

5 It will make a success of your life

To support Stephen Edoh's ministries, kindly forward your assistance to the PayPal address below:

PayPal: stephenedoh2000@gmail.com

PayPal.me/Stephenedoh

Six

Alignment

"Alignment is the act of following up, seeking, and holding tightly to a mandate along with putting order in place, so as to catalyse one's commitment and understanding towards success." – Stephen Edoh.

No successful organization, company, industry or institution ever got to the level of exploit without alignment.

In life, sometimes we fall out of understanding the fact that, without aligning ourselves to our visions, our dreams, we walk on to a new dawn, but it flashes away from our reach.

The simple truth about alignment is that, it helps an individual to be focused and be steadfast.

You aim towards being the best in your department, workplace, etc. But are you aligned with your target? This question is what makes the difference.

When you can't follow up with your vision, you'll experience a friction that will then cause a discord in you, in your personal life that will conflict with your dreams.

Alignment is significant in all dimensions of life. Without alignment, there will be no positive effect on one's vision, and where there is no vision, people perish.

Have you experienced a situation whereby after getting a task done, you find out that you didn't do the right thing? Sometimes you even argue with the results only to realize a while later that you weren't aligned.

" The moon has no light of itself, it simply
aligns at a proper position to the sun" — David
Oyedepo

Every minute of your life is very much important. We must learn to use each of the minute to fulfil a purpose, which will keep us on track to a new dawn.

"When we learn to align ourselves, we learn to be in order with our goals and aspirations." – Stephen Edoh. A man whose life is aligned is compared to a tea containing chocolate, milk and sugar. Do you comprehend? Everything required for tea was
available and was also put in place orderly. Same must be applicable to our lives too.

We must act in accordance with some relevant guiding tips, before we can be effectual in our walk to a new dawn.

Let's look at a few tips that will bring your life on the path of alignment:

1.Character 2.Vision
3.Execution

CHARACTER

"The results of every individual on earth depend on

their character." – Stephen Edoh.

Character is a distinguished feature that is found generally in every living beings. It is our character that defines our identity, personality, relationship and of all, it is character that determines the outcome of our life. Alignment is a basic tool for developing your character's identity.

The simple fact about humans is that no two persons have the same character or way of life or pattern of doing things.

Character is developed gradually from either a clean thought or a dirty thought. It's the thought that begets character, and character begets expressions.

In life, we must learn to always align ourselves with thoughts that are godly and positive, else, we put an end to our journey to a new dawn.

We are either the subject of negative thoughts that define us or positive thoughts that tell us who we truly are, in person.

The good and bad occurrences that we experience in our day to day life are clear results of character being displayed by people around the world.

Character could either be good or bad. It is our choice, which we want to adopt.

But you should always remember that, among the two types of character you are about to read on, one pays positively and the other negatively.

I affirm to the fact that nothing pays like being of good character, in all your ways. The book of proverb 3 vs 4 RSV makes it clear: "You will find favour and good repute in the sight of the Almighty God and also in the sight of men."

Let's visualize deep into the two basic dimensions of character.

Good Character

The word "Good" implies altruism, respect for life and a concern for dignity of sentient beings. When an individual adopts a change that seems pleasant and becomes subjected to that change, he or she begins to experience the newness of life.

The path to a new dawn is full of obstacles, storms and challenges. Character plays a vital role in conquering the storms of life, walking through the travail, also building a platform for understanding time and seasons with the ability to keep fighting.

No individual can triumph over the storms of life if he or she isn't subjected to a good character. A good character builds you, strengthens you and transforms you into a genius.

It's a matter of great honour and privilege when you act positively and in a unique way to some extent because, it draws feelings of admiration and respect from peers.

We can only achieve our goals, targets, dreams, ambitions, and vision when we allow our mind, spirit, body and soul to be guided by a good character. The benefits of engaging your mind with the goodness of spirit speaks not only for a moment but for an entire generation.

Great men like George Washington, Nelson Mandela,

John Wesley, Benson Idahosa, and even our Lord Jesus Christ lived a life that defines good character, and hence their names will forever remain alive for generations to come.

How to develop a Good Character

•Learn to work on your thoughts, i.e. always embrace positive thinking and views, and pack away any negative thought from your life.

•Avoid things that could corrupt your mind. You must avoid them irrespective of their worth.

•Your association with people must be positive and godly.

•Adopt a new lifestyle. You must keep watch and pray that you don't fall to the temptation of committing something evil.

•Become a friend of Jesus.

Evil Character

"Evil" implies hurting, oppressing, and killing others.

Men and women like A. Hitler, Queen Jezebel, Sani Abacha etc. paid the price for the wicked and evil character they chose to act on.

We see what's happening around the world today, especially in the South east countries of Asia and Western countries of Africa. Terrorism has become the major evil in these regions, but it's unfortunate and surprising that, these occurrences didn't just appear from nowhere. These were born out of the evil character of the people living in those regions.

When you apply a wrong formula in solving an equation, you end up failing. Same goes for adopting an evil or a negative character. In life, we often see people suffer, but sometimes it's not due to the high rate of unemployment in our society, corruption in democracy, lack of education, poor connection and accessibility to relevant information, but it is due to poor character.

Over the years we've heard of situations where the government of nations around the world sacked workers in various departments. Among these victims, you'll find bread winners who have others depending on them apart from their families. But the unfortunate and flabbergasting thing is that, their character cost them their job. What kind leads to such sorrow news? A bad one.

No path leading to greatness, was ever walked upon with a bad character. The fact that armed robbers take up their guns and end up having success in an operation doesn't mean they wouldn't pay the price at a certain time in life.

The Bible says in the book of Galatian 6:7 RSV "Do not be deceived; God is not mocked, for whatever a man sows, that he will also reap." This verse clears the air concerning what will happen to those in the position of carrying negative tasks. So, the fact that the police didn't apprehend the robbers yet doesn't guarantee continual success for those robbers, because, the day of penalization is coming up where they will reap all the evil they've sowed.

Evil character is a replica of the term sin. Religiously speaking, sin is the violation of moral or religious law. Sin defines wrong doing, walking on the wrong path, misusing the rules.

One of the major enemy of alignment is sin. When we walked out of the right path and into the wrong path, we subject our lives to sin and become subscribers of negative thoughts developing into negative character. Sin pushes us out of alignment, separate us from the will of God; and when we are separated from the will of God, we are subject to errors leading to the perishing of our lives.

When we leave the path of holiness, sin becomes our identity. Our lives turn upside-down while will walk in sin. We must exclude every sinful thought, behaviour, identity and patterns from our life if we want to avoid condemnation. Roman 8:1 RSV says, "For there is therefore now no condemnation for those in Christ Jesus." We must avoid sin, else we become victims of condemnation.

An individual whose life is ruled by sin, experiences nothing good other than the benefits of the flesh. Roman 6:23 RSV says, "For the wage of sin is death, but the free gift of God in Christ Jesus as our lord is eternal." The fact that you see corrupt people living luxuriously doesn't mean they aren't dead. Remember Rom 8:5: "For those who live according to the flesh set their minds on the things of the flesh, but those who live according to the Spirit set their minds on the things of the Spirit" and also Rom 7:5: "While we were living in the flesh, our sinful passions, aroused by the law, were at work in our members to bear fruit for death." When you lived and operate under sin which is the definition of negative or evil character, we become dead men walking.

You must embrace goodness, honesty, holiness, joy and of all, the Holy Spirit, to avoid sin and fast track your journey into a new dawn.

Consequences of an Evil Character

•Evil Character has no profit.

•When you allow your life to be ruled by an evil character, your life creates a picture of error and failure.

- Sin being a pathway to which evil came, pushes one out of alignment.
- Sin makes a sinner a dead man walking.
- Sin stops your journey towards a new dawn.
- Sin creates barriers in our lives.
- Sin blocks the will of God from fulfilling His purpose in our lives.

Tips to conquer sins

- Repentance from known sin.
- Seek out the grace of God (Roman 6:14).
- Live a righteous life. Adopt righteousness.
- Be a friend to the holy.

VISION

Vision is a clear picture of our dreams, desires, aspirations, ambitions, targets etc.

"Life without vision, operate in friction." – Stephen Edoh

The basic and fundamental key to explore any horizon is vision. Vision opens up a page and alignment reviews the main points in that page.

When we align to a positive picture in our heart, we create an easy route to our destiny. Vision is the lens of success. It views our imagination, opens us to our aspiration and steers us to the path of a new dawn.

I often hear people say they want to be famous, rich etc. But the missing key, which they still do not have access to, is vision. When you lack vision, you can't think, imagine or visualize anything positive, because, it is vision that brings out the blue print of your future.

I remember my first day as a pre-degree student at Benue State University. I visualized my future that very moment, feeling optimistic that at the end of the pre-degree program, I will become a medical student.

I worked hard and aligned myself, so that I would be able to bring forth what I visualized. To God be the glory, today, I'm a medical student, currently studying Human Physiology at College Of Health Science, Benue State University, Makurdi, Nigeria. But all of this became a reality when I decided to align myself to my vision.

Do you find yourself in a situation where you don't know your calling? Don't panic, I will provide few tips here which will help you realize your calling, align to your calling and produce results which that very calling signifies.

Let's look at those relevant tips:

1.Prayer

2.Observation

3.Striving

4.Sound mind

Prayer

Earlier, I made it clear that when you pray, your choices are being reviewed by the head of the realm; you're consulting.

"Therefore I tell you, whatever you asked in prayer, believe that you have received it and it will be yours", Mark 11:24 RSV.

Jesus is our lord and saviour, our role model, of all, he's our king. When we go to pray, the Holy Spirit opens us to a new realm, reviews Christ to us and gives us a clear understanding of the supernatural.

In prayer, we open up to our vision and callings through the help of the Holy Spirit. It is the Holy Spirit that calls men into various kingdom's ministerial offices, gives a kingdom's men words and utterances, boldness and security, wisdom and knowledge etc.

When we go to pray to the Father, through our lord Jesus Christ, with the help of the Holy Spirit, our prayers are answered. So whenever we go before God in prayer, whatever the problem might be, the Holy Spirit leads us in our intercession ensuring we get result as the end. Like apostle James said in Jam 1:5 RSV, "If any of you lacks wisdom, let him ask God, who gives to all men generously and without reproaching, and it will be given to him." This same verse applies to calling. We were not sent to earth without a purpose, but, with a mission; like he told prophet Jeremiah in Jeremiah 1:5: "Before I formed you in the womb I knew you, and before you were born I consecrated you; I appointed you a prophet to the nations."

Always adopt the habit of praying, because with prayers, a new dawn becomes a reality.

Observation

"The best way to discover the mysteries behind any
success story is through observation." – Stephen Edoh

Observation is essential in science. Scientists use observation to collect and record data, which enables them to construct and then test hypothesis and theories. Scientists observe in many ways – with their own senses or with tools such as microscope, scanner or transmitter to extend their vision.

No human on earth is endowed with one particular gift. God has deposited in us so many gifts, but it takes observation to discover them. In life, you will encounter different individuals with diverse talents. He or she could be a dancer, a singer, a writer, an artist, a footballer, etc.

At times we notice some individuals envy their talented peers, some even go beyond the boundaries, embracing jealousy, which is bad. The truth is that God wasn't impartial when he deposited the gifts he wanted in our lives. Some people feel like, why is she or he talented and I'm not. But the question of observation never comes across their minds.

Whenever you get yourself involved in a task, it is advisable that you pay maximum attention on yourself. Be a specialist in your day to day doings, check out where you're making great attempt, also where you're not doing that good. You will come to know more of your hidden ability, when you lens through your doings on a daily basis.

During this period of observation, you'll find out that you're overloaded with so many gifts. Until this very moment, you will find yourself being prudent in some dimensions. You will begin to notice the hidden abilities in you of which you are gifted with: an awesome voice, great writing ability, beautiful drawing skill, sound leadership mind-set, creativity etc.

Now, having discovered your calling, it is advisable you go get knowledge concerning your calling. Learn as much as you could, watch videos, listen to great men who have been there before you and always remember to strive!

It sometimes seems slower and time consuming in discovering your vision or calling, but you have to be patient and aligned.

"Do not despise these small beginnings, for the Lord rejoices to see the work begin." - Zechariah 4:10

Striving

Striving is the act of trying, making strenuous efforts with a persistent mind-set, in order to achieve a goal.

Individuals are opened to their vision when they allow the term 'strive' into their lives.

Thomas Edison kept striving even while the odds were against him. What could have been the implication today? Did it mean he gave up after making so many attempts on his proposed bulb hypothesis? Hmm… The world could still be searching for an antidote in counteracting darkness.

Having observed yourself, knowing your potentials and capabilities, you need to strive. In a case when you've discovered your calling, you don't just sit down and talk about it. Get up and begin to work on that vision, doing all that you know, positively, for that vision to become a reality.

It takes more to be a visionary in life. The big picture in our heart is being driven by the level of determination we are endowed with.

Our ambitions, goals, desires, dreams are the big pictures that streamline in our heart. These pictures only turn out to be the pretty movie everyone will ever wish to watch, only when we strive and make it clear that we won't give up.

Striving trains our mind, spirit and soul for greatness. It opens us to understand the struggles of life, the storm behind getting finance etc. When you are striving to be great, you put yourself on path, that mediocre can't step on.

Abraham Lincoln kept striving to become the president of the United State of America for more than two decades after failing many contests. He didn't give up. His dream was to lead his people to greatness. History made it known that Abraham Lincoln became the 16th president of The United States of America, and today he is regarded as one of the greatest president in the history of the United States of America.

Don't give up, now that you have just started the journey in making your vision a reality. Even when the odds speak against you, be strong, be brave and align yourself to ensure your vision becomes a reality.

Sound mind

"What differentiates a man from a boy is his mind-set."

– Stephen Edoh

The mind houses several countless things, in and out of the body. It's inside the mind that our thoughts develop, transform and then turn out to be a realistic expression.

Vision is at first acknowledged in the mind before other alignment processes come in. Your mind-set defines how far your vision will go, turning out to be a reality.

When our mind is not in alignment with our vision, we become sightless. Our mind must be sound, rigid, uncompromising and, of all, courageous.

A sound mind never errs, it stands still on a solid rock. You can't find a mediocre having a sound mind, because inside, it is empty.

Sound mind is meant for an optimist, not a pessimist; for hardworking people and not lazy people.

Being sound is a unique, pretty, admirable and awesome feature. A sound mind defeats fear, anger, slumbering etc.

My Bible made it clear to me that He hasn't given us the spirit of fear, but of sound mind.

Fear has stopped many individuals from becoming what they ought to have been today.

In our daily life, we encounter people, who are very talented, skilled, enthusiastic and prudent but what kills them is fear. Some of them are scared of trying because their thoughts are about failure, while others are scared due to their mind-set, concerning the fact that, famous people are being attacked and killed.

You could see talented footballers in the street, but when you go close to them, are they still there? Some of them, reply this way: "Most footballers are cultist and when you refuse to belong to a cult, you will die." This answer results from ignorance.

You have to deal with any form of ignorance, get rid of sluggishness in knowledge and poor vision.

Be brave, never allow anyone say those depressing words to you, but rather speak to yourself positivity, "I will always win, I'm not a failure, success is my story, I'm moving from zero to hero, my days of joy start now, I'm light and I will shine forth in every darkness." Remain sound, because it is in soundness that the meaning of your vision is reviewed to you.

To support Stephen Edoh's ministries, kindly forward your assistance to the PayPal address below:

PayPal: stephenedoh2000@gmail.com

PayPal.me/Stephenedoh

III

The phase of exploitation

Seven

Exploits

Daniel 11:32 KJV

And such as do wickedly against the covenant shall he corrupt by flatteries: but the people that do know their God shall be strong, and do exploits.

Every man on earth was created to rule, enjoy and do exploits-Stephen Edoh

It is very important to note that, exploit is very significant in all dimensions of life. No individual either in the secular or gospel world would prefer to remain inferior, but rather excel in their doings.

Exploit is the act, to which one takes advantage of knowledge, time, and wisdom, in alignment with a vision to produce heroic and extraordinary deeds, also to have one fast-tracked to a new dawn – Stephen Edoh A poor man thinks, an average man suggests, but a rich man does exploit.

You need to understand that, you're not here on earth purposeless, but on an assignment to fulfil a heavenly mandate placed on you, but exploit is what you need.

In life, there are three separate dimensions; The phase of struggle, the phase of restructuring and finally the phase of exploits. In our everyday life, we notice the struggles some people face, the pain they go through. It's quite unfortunate this sets of people travail, to afford a per meal.

We all know life is a struggle, we all want to enjoy, feel happy and live a luxurious life. But have you found time asking yourself, if you are visionary, ambitious or making an effort to be great? These questions are what make the difference.

In biblical times, many people did exploits and we shall be talking about someone, in particular, Joseph.

The Bible made us it clear to us that, Joseph as first was loved most by his father, but was hated by his brothers who later stole him into slavery. We came to understand that even while in Egypt, the country he serves, favour located him.

Favour is an identity of exploits. It is the physical and emotional manifestation of dominance. When an individual is favoured, it's implied that grace is upon him or her. Men and women of favour are doers of exploits. Joseph becomes the custodian of Potiphar's house because he was highly favoured. His exploit's caught the attention of his mistress, who lusts after him, only to have herself request of him, sex. It's didn't went in his favour, the Bible made it known that he rejected her wants, only to see himself land at the Prison yard after she lied to Potiphar his master.

Even while in prison, he was made Head over all prisoners, and they all were under his custody. But a time came in the prison, were two in-mate dreamt at night, but found themselves in a state of complexity, because the both of them, couldn't figure out what the dreams mean to them.

But this young man, favoured, salt seasoned, and designed for exploits, interpreted their dreams – of which one was pardoned and the other was executed.

Years later, still being the custodian of the prison, Joseph was forgotten by the in-inmate who was pardoned. But a moment came, when the number one citizen of the then Egypt, Pharaoh, was caught up at night, by a dream he found strange.

No magician, seer, Fortune teller, or wise men in the land of Egypt could interpret the dream, only for the pardoned servant of the king, to be brought to remembrance he has forgotten Joseph and needed to seek his assistance.

Joseph being God-led was presented before the king, with the magicians and wise men, all in attendance. By grace, he interpreted King Pharaoh's dream.

Pharaoh, now satisfied with the interpretation of the dreams he has, promoted Joseph from being the custodian of a prison to the rank of a prime minister.

What will have been the result, has it mean, Joseph slept with his master's wife, I guess he would have remained a slave till death. During intimacy, the father built you, equipped

you also prepares you for exploits – Stephen Edoh

Many haven't succeeded in doing exploits, due to the fact that they failed to acknowledge their creator, God.

It is very important to note that, seeking God in every direction of life, profit not only for a moment but an entire lifetime. So, therefore, you must have a good relationship with God, before you set for your journey to exploits. Let's explore more about the father.

Trust

Psalm 125:1 KJV

They that trust in the LORD shall be as mount Zion, which cannot be removed, a but abideth forever.

Trust entails an assured reliance on the character, ability, strength, or truth of someone –Merriam Webster dictionary.

What makes a relationship real and alive is trust. Your trust should define the father to be trustworthy. You must our trust in God, because he never fails, nor forsake but fulfil promises.

A very successful marriage is defined by the level of trust that exists between the couples. Same too goes to various workplaces, the level of trust that exists within the staffs will determine how aligned they are.

Trust is the seal of every intimacy. It's secured a relationship, built it upon a solid rock, also make that same relationship flourish.

The father is so much concerned and opened when you're willing to put all your trust in him. He's ready to be your fortress, your light, and salvation. Also, he will make you stand firm like Mount Zion, that can never be moved nor shaken, only when your whole trust is on him. Exploits is an occurrence that happens from the mind before a manifestation happened physically. The level of trust, you have towards the father, determine the level of your dominance.

When you walk in truth, people not only love you but do trust you as well. Trust is an evidence of love.

Without trusting God, the reading, studying and the meditation of the word cannot be effective.

So, therefore, always put your whole trust on God, because it is the beginning of exploits.

Benefits of trusting the creator

•Trusting brings about divine direction.

(Psalm 71:1 KJV. In thee, O LORD, do I put my trust: let me never be put to confusion.

•God Protect Those That Trust Him.

(Psalm 91:2 KJV. I will say of the LORD, He is my refuge and my fortress: my God; in him will

I trust).

•God Make Provision For those who trust Him.

(Psalm 37:3 KJV. Trust in the LORD, and do good, so shalt thou dwell in the land, and verily a thou shalt be fed).

•Trusting God Makes One Flourish.

(Psalm 52:8 KJV. But I am like a green olive tree in the house of God: I trust in the mercy of God forever and ever).

The word of God

Hebrews 4:12 KJV

For the word of God is quick and powerful, sharper than any two-edged sword, piercing even to the dividing asunder of soul and spirit, and of the joints and marrow, and is a discerner of the thoughts and intents of the heart.

The word!!

The word of God is the secrets of God. It opens you up to know more about the creator. It is in the word, we all come to discover that God is good, holy, supreme, merciful, etc.

When you make studying of the word a habit, you begin to act, think, behave and work as God.

Men who understood, work and act according to the word are doers of exploits, Daniel is a good example.

The word is alive and powerful, just like the above scripture said, also sharper than two-edged swords. Wow this scripture alone, already made it clear that with thee word, you are a conqueror, a dominator and a master planner of exploits.

Constant meditation and adherence to the word, is a mystery behind certain unexplainable success, we see today in people's lives.

It's quite unfortunate that some people take thee Bible which is the word of God to be boring. But the surprising thing about the Bible is that it is the oldest book with the latest news. The Bible book of Joshua made us understand the effects of the word, in it, chapter one verse eight, " Joshua 1:8 KJV

This book of the law shall not depart of thy mouth; but thou shalt meditate therein day and night, that thou mayest observe to do according to all that is written therein: for then thou shalt make thy way prosperous, and then thou shalt have good success ".

The word produces remarkable results, that can't be withstood by human intellects. We must accept the word, obey the word and watch the results, the word produces.

It's paid, having the word of God in you.

Excellence

For you to operate at the level of effulgence, in any dimensions of life, the spirit of excellence must be effective in your life – Stephen Edoh.

Excellence is the quality of being exceptional, creative, smart, intelligent, and of all, it is the state of being extremely good.

I will recall, to the fact that all human are meant to be doers of exploits. But indeed the topic of excellence must be reviewed.

An individual can be excellent in his or her way when they adopt the spirit of excellence. This entails the uniqueness, smartness, diligence and creativeness nature found in an individual.

The spirit of excellence stirs you up, opens you to a new dimension and give to you, the keys of exploits.

Excellence position, align and drives you to success. Without excellence, you will miss your way to success.

We all know the function of the hook, line, and sinker. Ask a layman, to tell you the function of the hook, line, and sinker, his response will be this way " well they are used for harvesting fishes ".

But that's not true, because the hook, line, and sinker are three different things. The hook performs the function of harvesting fishes, the sinker creates stability for the hook to carry its task perfectly and finally, the line creates the bond between the hook, sinker and indeed the fisherman. So, therefore, it's the hook that harvests the fish, not the line or the sinker, but indeed the hook won't fulfil its purposes without the support of the line and sinker.

So what am I trying to say? You need the spirit of excellence to triumph, excel and dominate. Because when you engaged your unique nature, creative ability, intellects, and persistence, you begin to experience the results of excellence in your life. But when you do otherwise, the results differ.

There are four dimensions that open, align and position an individual for excellence.

Let's explore!!

1. The mental state

Speaking on the mental state, of any homosapiens, demands a review on the mind; it structures, stability and function.

People who excel have no cockroach in their cupboard, nor skeleton in their wardrobes. They are clean-minded.

An individual who aspires to excel must adopt a positive mind-set, because the stability of the mind, depends on the physiological and anatomical nature of their thoughts, made by that individual.

Our thoughts beget our expressions. So, therefore, we must train our mind to bring forth positivity out of our lives.

It's advisable, individuals balanced the mental phase of their life, because of any errors from that very phase, cause a negative shift and also there will be a disorder in the life of that Individual.

So, therefore, the simple pendulum of the mental phase must be balanced because success starts with the thoughts we made.

2. The social phase.

Being social demands exposure.

Exposure injects excellence into the life of an individual. During the period of exposure, an individual comes in contact with new people, learn new cultures, also sail into new dimensions.

Being noteworthy, every individual who has gotten a six-grade education has been subjected to exposure.

Our lives have been designed to function in various dimension, but exposure makes it a reality.

Firmly speaking, you will never explore any dimension or do exploits, if you camp yourself indoor. Because exploits become an occurrence when the term " exposure " comes in.

Take, for example, an individual who aspires to become an actor stays indoor at all time. Will this dream ever come through? No!

As you subjugate yourself out to exposure, you begin to learn new things, become accessible to the latest information concerning your dreams, also get equipped with knowledge concerning other cultures.

It's the social phase, that opens you to know more about your dreams and aspirations, also helping you to do exploits with them.

Once you become exposed to the world, the keys to success step on your palm. How do I mean? Success is everywhere, you just need to go get it and the steps to get it results from being exposed.

Go exposed yourself, because it is the key to exploits.

The educational phase.

Legendary Nelson Mandela once defines education as a power tool, that could be used in changing the world.

Firmly speaking, I stand with that fact that says, education is the only tool used in conquering every dimension in this jet age.

The education phase in the life of every individual must be balanced, to ensure that limitation in progress is avoided.

You will only be a success when you get yourself educated. Aside from your field of study, it is of a commendable fact, when you find time reading, studying and exploring into other fields in the education sector.

I find the time, reading books pertaining to art, engineering, grammar, religion, history, etc. But I'm a Human physiology student, do we in any way relate ?? No, but no knowledge is waste.

The Educational phase, demand of us striving to learn things, that are still not known by us.

Every individual out there, must dominate their Hypothalamus with knowledge and introduce new things to their body internal environment, in other to do exploits.

Get a good education, and watch your life experienced nourishment.

Dominion

Dominion defines a state of having total authority to rule, subdue, conquer, also taking charge of life affairs.

Today, if you go around the universe, asking if anyone would prefer to be dominated, their answer certainly will be, No!. Because everybody wants to dominate, none want to be inferior but superior.

We all know that life is not the bed of roses, but a battlefield. So, therefore, we need to take charge, to dominate.

Dominion is a conquering force, that makes you reign on high. Men and women of dominance are doers of exploits.

We were created to go subdue portals, territories, nations and every dimension of life. But indeed, we were never created to be subdued nor dominated.

Dominance is our second name, we have been designed to take charge, to control, to rule, to occupy, to subdue. So, therefore, we must understand that the keys of exploits, the keys of portals, the keys of nations, the keys of doors are in our palms.

Dominion is being in control of affairs of life – David Oyedepo.

Let's study the key factors that will put us in charge;-

*Hard work

*Dynamism

*Striking

Hard work

To win a battle, you must have trained for long – Stephen Edoh

Having dominion isn't a day job, you have to go get it.

The laws that governed success, tip hard work to be one of its fundamental factors.

The struggles of life, are been overcome by hard work. Learning to work hard, is learning to position yourself for success.

Dominion is manipulated by hard-work. We lived in a time, were only those who work hard, survived starvation.

The ancient Roman's and Greece's subdued nations, because they were hardworking people. Not only that, history made it known to us, that technology started in this region. Due to the fact of hard work, the Romans and Greece's were mighty men of war, subjugators and men who were learned.

If you must take charge, then you must work hard – Stephen Edoh.

Hard work strengthens you for battles, its equipped your spirit man with courage and put you in the best position for the accolade of life. Go search the web, you will realize with no doubt, that the richest men of today, worked so hard to arrived at exploit.

Work hard and see your self dominate!!.

Dynamism

Dull people don't take charge, only smart and sound people does that – Stephen Edoh Soundness, loudness, and smartness are the keys, dynamic person use in taking charge.

Stop being dull, be smart and sound. You won't take charge with a dull mind-set.

Every born leader, dominators, subjugators, executors are product of sound, loud and smart minds. The sound mind makes you fearless, the loud mind turns you fiercer and the smart mind takes you through your way.

So, therefore, you must prepare to face the struggles of life with dynamism, at any given time. Because every prosperous man on earth passes through this stage.

Men like David were sound, loud, and smart. And these very features help them throughout their lifetime. David subdued nations because he was sound in all his ways. Even before then, his exploits started back then as a shepherd boy, killing a lion and a bear.

Dominance is an occurrence, that starts from the inside before manifesting physically. You must dominate yourself before you think of dominating the world.

Dominion put you in control of success. Aspire to dominate from this very moment, because men and women of dominance are champions.

Striking

When a blacksmith strike, our six tenses have it understood, that an effect is experienced that result in a new change.

Life is about striking to meet up with the relevant needs.

Our lives must be a replica of the blacksmith, in terms of consistent striking.

Striking is a key to exploit. No room for a lazy person in the chambers of dominators.

While you strike, you keep fighting, aiming for the best of life, with a mind-set of a dominator. There must be a consistent fight in your quest to have dominion.

You have been designed to occupy a domain in this life, to rule and govern dimensions of life. Dominion is your birth right, you have to take it by force.

You can't be dominator and lives in poverty, No!!.

Poverty knows its boundaries. It's respect those with power and authority.

So, therefore, it's time you go have dominion to champions affairs of life, as we journey into the beauty phase.

Summary

1.The word is full of life, its entrance is the beginning of a new dawn.

2.Excellence aligns and positions an individual for exploits.

3.Dominion is our birth right. So, therefore, we
are entitled to enjoy the things of life, subjugate nations and take charge

To support Stephen Edoh's ministries, kindly forward your assistance to the PayPal address below:

PayPal: stephenedoh2000@gmail.com

PayPal.me/Stephenedoh

Eight

Beautiful morning

The Earth gets brightened by the sun that rises from the East each beautiful morning. We feel calm and happy by the brightness of the day.

As each day walked by, we all get involved in one activity and the other; Some go juggling, others hang around, while some carry out their domestic chores.

The Beautiful morning is a clear picture of a new dawn. Think of its magnificent sunshine that brightens the day, its friendly weather that creates a fantastic atmosphere and the cool breeze that stirs the homeostasis, etc. Everyone would love to experience such moments.

I remember waking up that beautiful morning, years back in high school. We've just rounded up an academic session, of which the day before, was the end of the session ceremony. I've just claimed the prize for the best student in Chemistry and Biology. Imagine the joy that runs through my nerves. At last, I reaped the fruit of my labour. At that moment I exclaimed it is a new dawn.

It's unfortunate, many wake up daily only to experience a catastrophe. We sometimes pity them, maybe because of poverty, or a poor state of peace in their home, etc. But have we trace to their root, to find out if these cabals passed through the phase of struggle and also the phase of restructuring? This question makes a difference. It took a lot of time for you to get to this point, not forgetting your journey through the phase of struggle to the phase of restructuring, down to this very phase of exploit.

Now walk with me as I continue my journey. Every individual is destined to enjoy, to witness a beautiful morning, to be happy and of good cheers. The beautiful morning describes a moment life holds for exploits, success, good health, etc.

There are three major features of the beautiful morning, namely;

1. JOY
2. Peace
3. Victory

Joy

"Where there is light, there is joy," — Stephen Edoh

Joy is the end product of struggle, hard work, patience, etc. The Bible made us understand in the book of Psalm 30 vs 5 RSV, "Weeping may tarry for a night, but joy comes with the morning".

We are all destined to experience the fullness of joy in our lives. The beautiful morning of our life is first clouded with joy.

Joy, as I earlier said, is a product, an endpoint titre-value, and of all, joy is a result. If anyone aspires to live in joy, he or she must be ready to pay the price to sail to a beautiful morning.

The psalmist said, may those who sow in tears reaped in joy. The fact is this, no man or woman ever experienced joy without labouring, except he or she was born with a silver spoon. Think of those moments, where you travail in pain, walked through storms, faced beasts of various kinds, etc. All the struggles you went through earlier were all set up to put you through, in your walk to a new dawn.

Imagine the case of Hannah, who has been going to Shiloh, year after year, only for her to end with her Samuel. Think of those moments where she cries to the lord, imagine the wave of anguish that flies around the temple, at that tie. Eli, the priest, didn't understand all that was going on, only for him to call her a drunker. But the moment of joy came when she conceived her baby, after which she put to birth, a male child.

One of the major reasons that have stopped many from experiencing the fullness of joy is unnecessary hastiness. Some individuals are not patient, they just want to make success a reality by all means. Success isn't an occurrence resulting from coercion, you can't force it on yourself. It's only become a reality when an individual steps into a beautiful morning. Unnecessary hastiness will produce nothing good in life.

Think of joy as a strong Institution that supports a variety of healthy emotions, including happiness. The evidence of joy is general gratitude, contentment, optimism, a sense of freedom and other positive attitudes.

To grow in joy, we must resist not only self-pity but also being self-centred and self-absorbed. For joy to flourish, we must focus on showing love to others, because this is a mystery in experiencing a beautiful morning.

One key to experiencing joy is

God's Spirit. You can read below, on what Pastor Don Hooper said concerning the term Joy.

Supreme joy is God's nature and character! We see proof everywhere in God's creation — birds singing, animals leaping, flowers blooming, brooks babbling and the sun shining! Many people would be less depressed if they would spend more time outside. God "gives us richly all things to enjoy"

MYSTERIES BEHIND THE TERM JOY.

1. JOY IS A PROOF OF GOD'S LOVE TOWARDS

MANKIND

2. JOY IS A PRIZE, EVERY HARDWORKING INDIVIDUAL DESERVE.

3. JOY IS THE TRUE DEFINITION OF A NEW DAWN.

4. JOY RESULTS FROM A TURNAROUND IMPACT OF JOY.

1. JOY PROMOTE HAPPINESS

2. JOY CHANGES SITUATIONS

3. JOY STIRS THE HOMEOSTASIS

4. JOY IS THE SOUND OF VICTORY

My biggest wish is to remain joyous.

Stephen

Edoh

PEACE

"ASK A MILITARY PERSONNEL, WHAT IS

PEACE? HE OR SHE WILL ANSWER THIS WAY;

PEACE IS A STATE OF REST, ABSENT OF

VIOLENT AND PRESENT OF UNITY"

Peace is a concept of societal friendship and harmony in the absence of hostility and violence..

It begets progress, unity, harmony, dignity, etc.

One fountain of wealth is peace. With peace, an individual grows, communities progress and nations prosper.

The beautiful morning of life details peace as the mother of stability, the father of progress, promoter of unity.

Every successful man today, who is experiencing a beautiful morning, enjoys peace.

Peace is our portion!!

We don't have to struggle to have peace, because we have come to a phase of rest, joy, etc. None hate peace, except for an individual who is mentally retarded.

The fact is obvious if you seek and find peace, you will have peace.

The reason most people today don't experience peace in their home is because they didn't prepare, plan, and work hard. Unfortunately, it's doesn't work out for lazy people in this phase.

Now, walk with me, as I effect you, Knowledge.

WHAT MAKE PEACE A UNIQUE FEATURE?

1. PEACE IS A STABILISER.
2. PEACE IS A PROMOTER OF UNITY
3. PEACE IS A CATALYST FOR RAPID GROWTH IN OUR SOCIETY
4. PEACE BRINGS ABOUT COMFORT, CALMNESS AND REST.

VICTORY

ALUTA CONTINUA, VICTORY ACERTA.

They match started well for Manchester United, with Christiano Ronaldo hitting the net first. I was very happy to watch my team winning, until that moment when Frank Lampard stroke it hard for Chelsea FC. Honestly I felt cold. Minutes later, I get motivated, not just I alone, and other Manchester United fans around the globe. We went on chanting Ole! Ole! Ole! Ole! Ole! Ole! Ole! Ole! Ole, continuously till it was ninety minutes. They have declared none the winner, what a tough match? I exclaimed. The extra time kicks off, we didn't relax nor give up, but kept on motivating our team. It's was already an action of 120 minutes, yet none has been declared the winner. Next was the penalty shootout. I couldn't forget closing my eyes praying for Manchester United victory. Hmm, finally Nicolas Anieka missed his shootout and the last player of ours scored, at last, we were crowned King of Europe, 2007/2008. Oh my!!! The most beautiful moment, I ever have as a young lad.

This brief memory just proved the above intense quote "Aluta continua, victory acerta". What does it entail? The struggle continues, victory is certain. The fact is clear, victory isn't a fake achievement, it is worked for.

But now, it has a different view. The story has changed. You're now in a different dimension. A new dawn of unexplainable victories. Victory is the joy, success, peace, and happiness that result from defeating an opponent or an antagonist. It results from hard work, persistence, and determination.

From the very start till this very moment, we've been talking about the beautiful morning of life. But we can't give out an evident fact about the beautiful morning of life without talking about Victory.

As first you were aspiring, you then took a grand step in drawing a blueprint and started planning. Later on, you execute. The concept is simple; you don't think of happiness when struggling, the only thing in your mind is a question, when am I going to leave this situation? But you already leave that phase, those moments of pain, etc. Now you're in a New Dawn; detailed by a beautiful morning.

Having paid the price, here comes a moment of victory, a period of celebration, a day worth remembering. Your struggles are now things of the past, you're a now a success in any endeavour's you embark on. You don't have to think twice, whether your victory is temporary? No! It's permanent because you've paid an enormous price to experience a beautiful morning.

Every door now opens to you, because you are victorious. Then you were a victim of struggle, but now you're a success that begat victories. It is your identity, emblem and victory is your name.

Perhaps maybe you failed sometimes in the past, but that's your past and we aren't talking about past life but the present, I mean now! The last clause of the above intense quote says, "Victory acerta" meaning victory is certain. Do you comprehend? Victory is now for real, it's now in effect.

Now to everyone reading this, don't accept those clichés, that victory is an occurrence of luck. That's not true beloved, it's worked for. You're now a child of victory, with a winning mindset, a dominator, a champion, a leader and of all, a Star.

Remember, this is a beautiful day that arose from a beautiful morning. Victory has been assured.

Go Win!

Go Explore!!

Victory is yours!!!!!

Facts About Victory.

* Victory results from hard work.

* Victory, mark's a new dawn.

* Victory is the champion's language.

* Victory is a mystery that birth out from the beautiful morning.

Impact Of Victory:

* It's prepares a winner for the next phase of life.

* It quickens the spirit of optimism in an individual.

* It is a reward for hard work.

* Victory is a proof of success that results from the bond between you, your struggles, and your belief.

Key Nuggets:

* You will only experience the beautiful moment of life when you put yourself on the right path, I.e. doing all you've learnt so far in the book.

* Going through diverse phases to arrive at this very dimension; the beautiful morning isn't an occurrence that results from a mistake. So, therefore, know this, you are in a new realm, detail by positivity.

* Remember, alignment is the key. Don't involve in anything that will act contrary to your goals.

* For you to experience success, then you have to prepare to sail far into the beautiful morning.

Summary Of A Beautiful Morning

1. A beautiful morning detail a moment, life chooses to reward those who have worked hard to get to the top.

2. life is beautiful, but we see the beauty only in a new dawn.

3. Joy is not just the characteristic of a beautiful morning, but a result that birth out of hard work.

4. We all will take part in the fullness of joy, but a lot is required; persistence, endurance, etc.

5. The rich enjoy today because they've sailed long to this very dimension: a beautiful morning.

This book was put in place for you by God, don't think you read it by coincidence, see it as a divine occurrence.

To support Stephen Edoh's ministries, kindly forward your assistance to the PayPal address below:

PayPal: stephenedoh2000@gmail.com

PayPal.me/Stephenedoh

Nine

Accolades

" When I started the journey to a new dawn, I didn't give up, and I earned an accolade " – Stephen Edoh

I remember in 2009. It was a beautiful morning, I and my team-mates were preparing for the final of the regional football tournament. I wasn't under pressure either, the year before we won the trophy. But this time around, it was going to be different due to the quality of players our antagonist possesses. Being the Captain then, I stood confidently, also was positive and optimistic that my team will win the trophy. To be God be the glory, we won!! Thanks to goals from the dual brothers; Valentine Ubah and Arinze Ubah. A memory worth remembering!!

An Accolade is an award or privilege granted as a special honour or as an

Acknowledgement of merit. Every dimension of life carries an accolade; for the best, hardworking, intelligent, etc. Take, for example, a child who did exploits in her academic performance, topping her class with the highest average of 95.0, how does the school management reward such a child? Oh my!! The average alone is mouth-wetting, she will end up with a prize, only because she paid the price.

For you to earn the prize, pay the price

Do you know why men like Albert Einstein won the noble prize? They pay the price. This was a man at the level of effulgence. A genius, an icon, a protagonist and an impact on generations. I will forever remember Albert Einstein for his notable contribution to science. Think of the quantum theory, the theory of relativities and many much more. Honestly, he paid a price that none in this generation could pay. Most people, especially those outside the field of science, don't really know the impact of the laws, Einstein proposed. A chemist knows how relevant the quantum theory is in chemistry. Same goes to the physicist concerning the fact of relevance when speaking on the theory of relativities. What am I trying to say? Every contribution, struggle, hard work is rewarded with an accolade. Like Einstein, He Won a noble prize.

Never think you won't be rewarded for the struggles you've gone through, for the good deeds you've done. There will come a time were you will be rewarded for your time and contribution. The fact is obvious, No lazy person ever received an accolade, because it's meant for winners.

The funniest aspect is this, some individuals envy their accolade-awarded peers. But why envy your peers? When you can win. What a disgraceful attitude found in the lives of many today. It happens to me in year two, while I was still in high school. I was spoken bad of, mocked, etc. Even when I did nothing. The fact is this, every accolade winner will attract friends and, enemies. Your struggles got you here, you have to be thankful to God who kept you alive, quickens you with wisdom to be calm and strengthens you, for you not to give up.

I smile each time things are working for my good. Do you know why? The reason is that whenever I'm struggling, I used to have it clear to myself that, "It's only for a while". You have the potentials, the chances, the speed, the talents, the ability, so, therefore, why sit down and watch your talents, abilities, potentials, chances, waste? Common stand up and make hay, while the sun still shines.

You're now in a new phase, a dimension meant to be walked upon only by winners. Your name has been changed, you now belong to the family of exploits. You aren't that dullard anymore, but a star.

Now walk with me, as I take a new direction. We are about to explore an extra dimension.

YOUR GOALS

In life, goals matters. Every individual want to be something great; a musician, newscaster, doctor, an engineer, etc. Goals are target, dreams, wishes, etc.

Setting of goals is the very first step an individual take towards earning an accolade sooner or later in the new dawn era. You must set your goals, not only that, also begin to aspire towards a bigger picture of that that goal you've set.

When individuals out there refuse to set goals, they act and behave like scalar quantity, without direction. It's important to note that, setting of goal is the first and one of the greatest steps on the stairs to a new dawn.

It's quite unfortunate many doesn't even knows how to set their goals, which sounds flabbergasting. Indeed, we are all student in the school of knowledge, so you're not expected to insult or mimic nor mocked an individual.

Let's look at the step in setting off goals.

HOW TO SET YOUR GOALS

1. Get a pencil
2. Write your goals, dreams, ambitions, etc. on a shit of paper.
3. Make a timetable and begin to work with it concerning your goals.
4. Dream big
5. Think big, and finally

6. Adopt a standard.

YOUR BLUE PRINT

Every building has blue print. The blue print detail about the house plan, how the building comes to be in existence, where it all started from, etc. Ask a football coach, what will be His or Her biggest dream ever? He or she will respond this way, "To be an Uefa champion's league winning coach or a Fifa world cup winning coach". But can this dream come true without a blue print? No!! Why? Because the foundation of every vision, dream, aspiration is the blue print.

all youth reading this chapter must have a blue print, for the thoughts of a greater tomorrow, to become a reality. Preparation matters, because when you refused to prepare for tomorrow, you will pay the price for laziness. Majority of the problems we experienced today in our day-to-day life, result from lack of preparation. That is why many graduate finish with good grade and still not get a job, why? Lack of preparation.

We must prepare for tomorrow, get our seat belt fastened and align to the right principle. I've put this very topic, to prepare you for an accolade. Because tactics and strategies are necessary factors for an accolade.

Earlier on, I spoke to you concerning time management, and alignment. These key factors are very significant in your walk to a new dawn.

Lack of preparation has become a major catastrophe in our nation. It's now a disaster for many families to pay their house rent, children's tuition, water-light bills, etc. But do you know what? Most of these people are sometimes reckless, when it's come to the topic of managing time and finance. As soon as money flows in, all they thought of his excitement, picnic, unnecessary outings, etc. This kind of lifestyle can't birth anything good nor produce any good fruit.

Lay a blueprint to lie on a blue-bed

Your goals need your plan to be fulfilled, like I said in the chapter titled, "Alignment". It's time you lay out the building block of your future, if you aspire to be great.

HOW TO lie DOWN THE BLOCK OF YOUR FUTURE

1. Create time for yourself and all the activities you engage in.
2. Find time working on yourself, learn news things.
3. Work on your vision. i. e. get the relevant knowledge related to your dream.
4. Align yourself.
5. Stay focused, embrace the spirit of excellence to be perfect.

A New Dawn—ACCOLADE

"When you apply laws or principles, you are likely to get the necessary result that law or principle holds for" – Stephen Edoh

Labourers get their wages at the end of every work done. Same applies with those who worked hard, get their reward. In this dimension, we shall be exploring more in reward.

Every tremendous work done deserve a credit, due to the level of effort inputted, the passion showed forth, and the level of patience act upon in getting a perfect result. It's a concept of sow and reap. There is no partiality here, you're rewarded according to the level of effort you invested into a work.

Accolades are for real, because many who haven't been an award winner for once, see it as a planned stuff or perhaps a thing of luck. But it isn't true, accolades are worked for.

Every true champion or aspiring leader should take this words of mine. "If you must keep the train moving, you have to keep fuelling it continuously". How do I mean by this statement? The train mentioned indicates your success, while the subordinate clause "You have to keep fuelling it" implies that, you have to keep striving, fighting, and striking to ensure, you remain at the top.

I'm so much happy, you've taken your time to read to this very point, because deep in me I sensed clearly that, your life has experienced a change that cause a shift in your destiny.

Remember, it is a new dawn, it is your time to be rewarded for your past struggles, travails, etc. The accolade I've for you is this book. You can share it around the globe.

TIPS THAT WILL HELP YOU CLAIM AN ACCOLADE

1. Draw the blue print of your success, because success begins from masterminding and planning.
2. View a big picture of yourself. i.e. Be sound and. Optimistic.
3. Think big.
4. Dream big. 5. Work hard.
6. Encamped around optimist.
7. See success as an occurrence and not a thing of luck.
8. Be desperate to win.
9. Align yourself.
10. And finally, Be you!!

KEY NUGGETS:

1. When we refuse to plan for an accolade, we prepare our lives for a breakdown.
2. Every principle and laws governing success must be obeyed and followed, to make an individual eligible for an accolade.
3. When you fail, change your mindset and try again. Because the walk to success start with optimism.
4. Never forget this, Alignment. Because it is a basic and fundamental key in exploring any horizon.
5. Always Be You!!

SUMMARY

1. Winning an accolade demands a lot from hard work.
2. Setting of goals is the first step in earning an accolade.
3. Blue print is the foundation of every dream, vision and goals.
4. Laws and principles governs success. So, therefore, every

individual aspiring for an accolade life holds, must obey and follow laws and principle.

5. Align yourself, else you go half way as you journey to a new dawn.
6. You will become who you want to be, if only you BE YOU!!

It is a new Dawn!!

To support Stephen Edoh's ministries, kindly forward your assistance to the PayPal address below:

PayPal: stephenedoh2000@gmail.com

PayPal.me/Stephenedoh

Ten

A remnant in His imperial Garden

"The numbers of civilization using their purpose in this age are fewer than we previously thought. We cannot afford to be outside the box because of the things God has in store for this generation and beyond." - Stephen Edoh.

In every generation, there is always a set of people who still believe and obey the Father's will throughout the ages. There are rarely majorities, but a minority group with a belief system citing their obedience to God as their number one priority. Yet even in their small numbers, they still exist as thousands.

As human beings residing on this planet known as Earth, we all subscribe to a certain belief system that guides and directs our thoughts. It is one reason why people from other parts of the world relate differently in almost every routine. More so, belief systems are unique because they bring out the way of life of a certain people, tribe, group, and even alliance.

The famous Merriam-Webster defines the word "remnant" as a small thing left over from the original thing. It could be a material thing, etc. But in this chapter, we're going to talk about the Christian version of who a Remnant is on the surface of the earth.

Let me bring you a definition I chose from the Oxford Advanced Dictionary I like. It defines the word-Remnant as a small minority of people who will remain faithful to God.

We are a Remnant of the Imperial Garden of the Divine. It is a fact that God has called us, in this time of existence, to fulfil a mission. It may surprise you that everyone on earth exists as an instrument that God wants to use. However, only a few end up being used by the Divine to fulfil the course of Celestial Sovereignty.

In the Father's grand Garden, our existence means more than we can ever say to the understanding of men. One thing I want you to infer is this: You are a remnant that God wants to use to fulfil His mission.

Why Does The Remnant Exist?

Hmm, the question above is one, many for years continue to ask, with some answers emerging. We will delve deeper into the subject to get to the point of our satisfaction regarding the question asked above.

TO PREVENT THE FALL OF A CULTURE.

"Human beings cannot exist where there is no culture." - Stephen Edoh.

At the beginning of this chapter, I made it clear on that which concerns human existence and belief systems. I also stated how a man is guided and directed by a belief system.

Sociology defines the word-Culture as a way of life of people, society, etc. Therefore, everyone has a culture which is referred to as their belief system.

The main reason why today we speak and write in the English language is that people in the past taught others how to communicate with this lingua Franca. It is the same way God calls us to be the Remnant of this last age.

Many of us learned the good virtue we exhibit today from our parents and teachers. God is calling us to do the same with our children and those under us. We must not allow the virtue of goodness and morality to die with us. Let us remember that attitudinal effects are contagious. If we teach children and adolescents the right things, they will surely grasp all the knowledge and transform our world for good.

The reason for the upheavals and turmoil in our world today is the existence of a terrible majority. We can all relate to the fact that bad people do not create a friendly atmosphere, nor do good people create a gloomy reality.

So while others mislead their generation, please decide in your own heart to inspire your generation towards good. This will not only earn you a legacy when you are long gone, but will pave the way for a personal crown made of gold.

TO INSPIRE A PURPOSEFUL TRIBE

"We were created by God with a purpose simply to fulfil His will here on earth."– Stephen Edoh.

If there is any man on the surface of the earth without a purpose, then that man is considered a living dead because everyone on earth has a purpose to fulfil throughout their time on earth.

To make this series interesting, I will share with you a short piece on the topic - Purpose from one of my authored books titled "A woman of honour" which you can get online. In that book, I discussed dating and how a purpose-driven relationship can improve an individual.

"At a certain stage in life, everyone needs to have a close friend in the other to soar to the top of the hill of life," - Stephen Edoh.

Purpose is an aim given to an individual, in others, for a translation to take effect from the Horizons of Zion. It is the exclusion of man's will and including God's will. More so, It is the difference between our calling and earthly desires. Our calling is being embraced by the very purpose we are here on earth to fulfil. While our earthly desires are pioneered by hard work, persistence, determination, and passion.

In a time and age when the whirlwind of life is blowing so hard on the earth's surface; it only takes one purpose for a woman of honour to know her position. The life of every woman of purpose is an interesting poem being read by pioneers and mighty subjugators of the age. What makes a lady, a woman of honour, is purpose. As a lady with a positive difference, her beauty and character are not all you need to make her yield to the hall of fame. What certifies her as a woman of honour is the realisation of purpose.

Any purpose-driven relationship fulfils the will of the Divine here on earth. One decision you must make before marriage is this: discover your purpose!

Dating is a platform that creates an atmosphere to unravel various things in the tale of life. Unfortunately, most relationships suffer from angst and setbacks because of a lifestyle known as free-riding. Jesus made an amazing statement in his day, "Many will come in my name", This same statement translates into many relationships; a man might conclude that he loves a lady, unfortunately, he is only sucking the sweet part of her nectar; deluding her into believing his fictitious actions. As a lady with a difference, be sane and spiritual in discerning the right man meant for you, otherwise, the hungry wolf in his polished regalia will eventually devour you.

A man's purpose must displace the trace of greed and selfishness in his relationship. All love associations that operate under the influence of greed take a little step backwards. Your life is not a gateway to someone else's success when you act like a former and not a reformer.

From what we have just read, it is clear how this reality we know as purpose can help displace the despised in every relationship.

We are called by God to raise people who will discover their purpose and fulfil the Father's will here on earth. It pleases God when He realizes that we do the things that are expected of us here on earth.

The Bible clarifies that parent must train his children in the Lord's way because it is the first key that opens the door of purpose. So, as parents and guide: mentors, and leaders; we are expected to lead in the way that pleases God. And when we do the right things, our chapter continues to add up forever in Eternity.

We are not just a Remnant on Earth, but a flower in His Imperial Garden. Our determination to accomplish other purposes, position us above the mediocrity in our world. It is a clarion call for all to rise and lead a purposeful team.

TO RAISE A PECULIAR PEOPLE

"One of our goals on earth is to raise peculiar people everywhere" - Stephen Edoh.

The Holy Spirit is prominent as an entity that helps Christians to raise anything that brings glory to the Divine. It could be in raising an altar, perhaps children. He is a powerful entity that perfects that dimension.

We are in a generation where the devil works tirelessly to ensure that every work that Christians engage in, fails. It is the reason why we need the Holy Spirit now more than ever.

There is no Christian on earth who can do without Him, because it is He who directs and guides our steps to the Father. And without an intimacy with the Father, our journey to the door of success will not materialise, unless we do the opposite by bowing down to the devil.

To be honest, nothing good can ever come out of the life of an individual who does not know the Holy Spirit. It is not a curse that I am putting on those who do not know the Divine. Besides, I am just stating the fact.

Like flowers of the Divine and a Remnant of His Imperial garden;

there is a call to each of us to raise a peculiar generation. It is not an assumption, as many would speculate, but the truth that God wants us to know.

A peculiar individual is one whom God has called to time to begin and end a course here on earth. It is a fact that peculiar people are distinctive before the eyes of all who cross their path. We need not to tell a man who peculiar persons are, because the aftermath of their actions speaks louder.

When we come across a peculiar individual, some realities birth out of their existence, and we will delve a little deeper into the subject as I have discussed them at length in my previous books. Stay tuned as we complete this series with a short but powerful message.

A MIGHTY ENTITY OF LOVE.

"Peculiar people are defined by one word-Love."-Stephen Edoh.

God did not create any man simply to see him live in the world's style. No! He created us to live a life that will bring Him glory throughout the ages. It is a fact that our existence is about the glory of God.

Our lifestyle either brings glory to God, perhaps, it brings shame to God. The devil is always pleased when we go against the ways of the Divine. More so, Satan wants us to be under his influence simply because it makes him feel superior to the Father, however, a blatant lie.

Every flower in the Oasis of the Divine is a powerful entity of love. We know well that love is a language that only powerful entities engage in to communicate their thoughts and feelings. You will not find people of the world engaging in, instead, they lust after mundane things.

One thing we must do at all times is this: we must love others and also teach those under and around us how to express the love of Christ. We must do this because we are the Remnant of this generation, and the next generation must feel our impacts.

When we treat others with love and teach those on our threshold to show love; our actions pave the way for a better world. On the other hand, if we cannot let love have the sayings in our lives and the lives of others, then we plan to have a world rocked by chaos and turmoil.

The reason we have weak leadership among us is that love has not been given the key to lead our world. In any nation where love is a minority, then wars and unrest become the main reality of the day.

Our Lord and Saviour, Jesus Christ made us understand in His words through the Apostles that love is the greatest of all virtues that man could ever subscribe to. Every time we subscribe to love, our actions invite happiness and the good things in life.

We know well that love does not boast of its outcome. It is a fruit of the Spirit of God and a virtue that cannot be defeated. Yes, love is a weapon! Any man who fights with love remains undefeated throughout the ages. This same love that led our Lord Jesus Christ to say, "esteem your neighbour's and enemies as yourselves".

Children who exhibit the virtue of love grow up to become a powerful entity in the hands of God. Many will think we are eye-serving whenever we express love to the sensation of others, but it is our identity.

Let love take us wherever we go because it is the greatest virtue that makes us who we are. Remember that no man is a flower of the Divine until love leads them.

–

We believe that this very chapter has blessed you. It will be an honour to receive help from you.

Stephen Edoh Ministries needs your partnership to continue to spread God's words to the nations.

We need your support. It could be a monthly help, maybe just a moment's help.

We will be glad and happy if you decide to help us.

You can send your partnership or one-time support payment through our PayPal email address below.

You can also testify to how this book has impacted your life using the same email below.

PayPal payment email address: **Stephenedoh2000@gmail.com**

Pay Pal link: **www.Paypal.me/StephenEdoh**

Thanks and many blessings to you and your family.

Culled from the book titled, "The Flower of the Divine" by Edoh Stephen Owoicho.

About the Author

Edoh Stephen Owoicho was born in Plateau State, Nigeria to a Benue indigent parents in the year, 1999. Whereas, he grew up in New Karu, Nasarawa State, Nigeria.

For many years he has been writing poems, articles, and songs. His first book, "A New Dawn," earn a recommendation, from many Nigerians and friends abroad. In 2019, he wrote his second book, "Woman of Honour, " which has turned out to be a blessing to many ladies in Africa and beyond.

Furthermore, He is a medical physiology student at the prestigious College of Health Sciences, Benue State University, Nigeria.

What more, He is the founder of Words Citadel Family; a spoken and written team who's goal is to stir, inspire and transform the lost and broken.

CPSIA information can be obtained
at www.ICGtesting.com
Printed in the USA
LVHW030737111121
702999LV00006B/346